5-15-13

Beyond War

ALSO BY DAVID ROHDE

Endgame: The Betrayal and Fall of Srebenica

A Rope and a Prayer: The Story of a Kidnapping
(and Kristen Mulvihill)

Beyond WAR

REIMAGINING AMERICAN INFLUENCE IN A NEW MIDDLE EAST

DAVID ROHDE

VIKING

VIKING
Published by the Penguin Group
Penguin Group (USA) Inc., 375 Hudson Street,
New York, New York 10014, USA

USA | Canada | UK | Ireland | Australia | New Zealand | India | South Africa | China
Penguin Books Ltd, Registered Offices: 80 Strand, London WC2R 0RL, England
For more information about the Penguin Group visit penguin.com

First published in 2013 by Viking Penguin, a member of Penguin Group (USA) Inc.

10 9 8 7 6 5 4 3 2 1

Page 221 constitutes an extension of this copyright page.

LIBRARY OF CONGRESS CATALOGING-IN-PUBLICATION DATA
Rohde, David, 1967– author.
Beyond war : reimagining American influence in a new Middle East / David Rohde.
pages   cm
Includes bibliographical references and index.
ISBN 978-0-670-02644-9
1. United States—Foreign economic relations—Middle East. 2. Middle East—
Foreign economic relations—United States. 3. United States—Relations—Middle
East. 4. Middle East—Relations—United States, I. Title.
HF1456.5.Z4M6287 2013
337.73056—dc23   2012039754

Printed in the United States of America
Set in Minion Pro with Chronicle
Interior and Map Designed by Daniel Lagin

To my daughter

CONTENTS

CONTENTS

PART II
A Way Forward

AUTHOR'S NOTE

For personal reasons, I limited my travel while researching this book. In 2008, two Afghan journalists and I were kidnapped by the Taliban outside Kabul, taken to the tribal areas of Pakistan, and held captive there for seven months. Out of deference to the concerns of my family, I have not traveled to Afghanistan, Pakistan, Libya, or Egypt since the kidnapping. A list of the many journalists whose reporting, insights, and analysis from those countries this book relies on is in the acknowledgments, endnotes, and bibliography. I am enormously grateful to them for their intelligence, bravery, and outstanding work. Any and all mistakes, errors, and omissions in the pages that follow are wholly my own.

The Middle East, North Africa, and South Asia

COUNTRIES THAT ARE THE FOCUS OF THIS BOOK

Switzerland
Austria
Hungary
Ukraine
France
Slovenia
Croatia
Italy
Romania
Bosnia and Herzegovina
Serbia
Bulgaria
ISTANBUL
Greece

Portugal
Spain

Morocco
TUNIS
Sidi Bouzid
Gafsa
TUNISIA
TRIPOLI
Benghazi
Alexandria

Mediterranean Sea

Algeria
LIBYA

Western Sahara

Mauritania
Mali
Niger
Chad

Senegal
The Gambia
Burkina Faso
Guinea Bissau
Guinea
Benin
Nigeria
Sierra Leone
Côte d'Ivoire
Togo
Ghana
Central African Republic
Liberia
Cameroon

INTRODUCTION

On September 11, 2012, the American ambassador to Libya and three other Americans were murdered. A bizarre American-made amateur video that portrayed the prophet Muhammad as a libidinous child molester sparked anti-American protests across the Islamic world. The conflict in Syria raged. And Israeli leaders talked of preemptive military strikes against Iran's nuclear program.

To Americans, the Middle East seemed as inimitably volatile, radicalized, and anti-American as it did on September 11, 2001. Despite the sacrifice of sixty-six hundred American lives in Iraq and Afghanistan and the spending of $1.2 trillion, the region seemed as unstable as ever. Reeling from economic problems at home, exasperated Americans wanted as little to do with the region as possible.

This book is an effort to describe a new, more pragmatic, and more effective American approach to the Islamic world. I believe that a more economic and less military-oriented effort will achieve more than the invasions of Iraq and Afghanistan did. In some instances, drone strikes, covert operations, and lethal force may be necessary, but investment, education, and normalized relations are equally potent weapons. We must develop a more multifaceted understanding and approach to the region.

The murders of Ambassador Chris Stevens and three other Americans in Libya were part of a historic struggle between moderates and hard-liners over the future of Islam. Its outcome will affect the United States, its allies, and the global economy for decades.

Intensive media coverage of violent anti-American protests distorts American views of the Arab Spring. The Arab world is not a monolith. Nor are the world's 1.6 billion Muslims. In the weeks after the murder of the four Americans, tens of thousands of Libyans protested against the killings, apologized to the United States, and demanded that militias disarm. In public opinion surveys, clear majorities in Egypt, Tunisia, Turkey, and Pakistan called for democracy and personal freedoms—and Islam—in political life.

The polling matched my experience in a decade of reporting across the region since 2001. Arabs and South Asians said they did not want to be dictated to by Americans. Nor did they want militants to impose an extreme version of Islam on them. Instead, they yearned for a third way where their countries could be both Muslim and modern.

In Tunisia, Libya, and Egypt today, young people long for American high-tech investments, trade, and education. Public opinion surveys show an admiration for American technology, pop culture, democratic ideals, and ways of doing business. They also show a deep suspicion of America's intentions in the Middle East and its commitment to democracy.

In its second term, the Obama administration should publicly ally the United States with Arabs and South Asians who support and abide by democratic norms, oppose violence, and uphold international human rights laws, whatever their faith. The core focus of

American policy in the region should be finding ways to quietly, consistently, and effectively strengthen those groups over the long term. The most potent long-term weapon against jihadists is moderate Arabs and South Asians, not American soldiers.

The process will not be easy. American policy makers must learn to differentiate among opaque organizations and movements. The Muslim Brotherhood and other Islamist political parties that won elections in Egypt and Tunisia are not ideal. But our true enemies—and theirs—are violent Salafist militants.

Across the region, twin imperatives should guide American policy. Terrorist groups should be targeted but economic growth must be fostered as well. Today 60 percent of the Middle East's population are under the age of thirty. If they are to be gainfully employed, more than 100 million jobs will need to be created in the region by 2020, according to the International Monetary Fund.

Change is also needed at home. Over the next four years, it is vital that the Obama administration revamps and revitalizes Washington's archaic foreign policy apparatus. From 2001 to 2009, I covered Afghanistan, Pakistan, and, to a limited extent, Iraq for the *New York Times*. During that period, Washington's outdated reliance on military force and its weakened civilian agencies severely limited its efforts. While numerous books have focused on the post-9/11 American military and intelligence efforts, the first half of this book will examine the over $67 billion the United States spent on civilian aid programs in Afghanistan, Iraq, and Pakistan. Between 2001 and 2011, tens of thousands of Americans implemented a civilian effort designed to promote economic growth, build infrastructure, improve governance, strengthen institutions, expand education and health care, foster civil society, and train local police, judges, journalists, and human rights advocates.

By almost any measure those programs produced meager results. Washington squandered billions, neglected its true allies in the region, and failed to employ its most potent nonlethal tools: American technology, consumerism, and investment.

Of the roughly $1.3 trillion the United States spent in Iraq, Afghanistan, and the global war on terror, 95 percent went to the American military effort. When civilian initiatives were mounted, sweeping changes that would take years at best to achieve were expected within months. And to an extent never seen before in American history, post-9/11 Washington relied on private contractors to achieve its goals and waged for-profit war.

At the peak of the wars in Iraq and Afghanistan in 2010, 46,000 American contractors and 214,000 third-country and local contractors worked for the American government in both countries. At times, American government contractors outnumbered American troops.

Congressional investigators later concluded that the use of contractors minimized the number of American troops and hid the wars' human toll. Between 2001 and 2011, 8,560 U.S. soldiers and contractors died in Iraq and Afghanistan. Of the dead, 28 percent were contractors. While newspapers across the country faithfully printed the name of each American soldier who perished, there has been no such listing of contractors.

At the same time, privatization proved to be wasteful. Investigators found that contracting was sometimes more costly than employing government workers, and tales of shoddy work abounded. All told, federal agencies paid a staggering $206 billion to contractors in Afghanistan and Iraq from 2001 to 2011. Investigators estimated that $31 to $60 billion was lost to waste, fraud, and abuse.

In Afghanistan, Pakistan, and Iraq, I met civilians, government workers, and contractors who were in pursuit of money, adrenaline, or escape. I also found well-intentioned civilians intensely frustrated by the American government's ill-suited strategies and tactics.

While working as a columnist for Reuters and the *Atlantic* in 2011 and 2012, I visited Turkey and post–Arab Spring Tunisia and saw opportunities to back moderates being squandered. There, and across the region, speed, visibility, and American political dynamics ruled. Patience, complexity, and deference to local cultures were shunned.

This book is a call for change. After analyzing the Bush and Obama administrations' civilian efforts in Afghanistan, Pakistan, and Iraq, it details the opportunities and risks that the rise of Turkey and the Arab Spring present.

In hindsight, Washington's unsuccessful civilian efforts in Iraq, Afghanistan, and Pakistan exposed the dangerously weak state of its own civilian institutions. In the decades since the end of the cold war, the ability of the White House, State Department, and Congress to devise and carry out sophisticated political and development efforts overseas has withered. And while the complexity of global challenges has increased, rising partisanship and a twenty-four-hour news cycle in Washington have fueled demands for quick, inexpensive resolutions that are illusory.

The use of contractors is a symptom—and a cause—of the decay in American civilian institutions. In all three countries and so far in the post–Arab Spring, the result on the ground has been a disjointed, wasteful, and largely failed civilian effort. In a volatile and rapidly changing region, there is a desperate need for a new American approach. This book describes it.

PART I
For-Profit War

CHAPTER 1

Little America

In the spring of 2004, a seventy-two-year-old American aid worker named Charles Grader told me a seemingly fantastical story. In a bleak stretch of Afghan desert that resembled the surface of Mars, several dozen families from states like Montana, Wisconsin, and California had lived in suburban tract homes with backyard barbecues. For thirty years during the cold war, the settlement served as the headquarters of a massive American project designed to wean Afghans from Soviet influence.

American engineers oversaw the largest development program in Afghanistan's history, constructing two huge earthen dams, 300 miles of irrigation canals, and 1,200 miles of gravel roads. All told, the project made 250,000 acres of desert bloom. The town, officially known as Lashkar Gah, was the new capital of Helmand province and an ultramodern world of workshops and offices. Afghans called it "Little America."

Intrigued, I hitched a ride to the town with Grader a few weeks later. A weathered New England blue blood, Grader was the last American to head the Kabul office of the U.S. Agency for International

Development before the 1979 Soviet invasion. In 2004, he was back in Afghanistan working as a contractor, refusing to retire just yet and trying, it seemed, to do good.

From the moment we arrived in Lashkar Gah, I was transfixed by Little America, its history and its meaning. At enormous cost, a sweeping American cold war effort had temporarily eased the destitution of one corner of Afghanistan but failed to achieve its loftier, long-term goals. Surveying the town, I desperately hoped America could do better now.

Instead, I would witness an epic tragedy that unfolded over the next eight years. Between 2001 and 2012, over nine hundred American and British troops died in Helmand—nearly twice as many as in any other Afghan province. At the same time, the U.S. and British governments spent billions of dollars in a desert province twice the size of Maryland with a population of only 1 million. Hundreds of highly paid foreign contractors arrived to train Afghan police, farmers, and government officials as well.

A clear pattern emerged in Helmand. When massive international efforts were made, real progress emerged. The provincial capital and other large towns in central Helmand grew more secure and thrived economically, and narcotics cultivation declined. But in isolated rural areas, poverty, corruption, and Islamic conservatism defied a scattershot approach.

On each trip, I met dozens of well-intentioned American and Afghan civilians trying to achieve those goals. But instead of triumphing, many of them ended up dejected, confused, and cynical. As American and British forces prepare to withdraw from Helmand in 2013, Afghans fear that the gains will crumble. The failures of Little America—and what they say about America's place, role, and future in the world—haunt me as well.

* * *

In 1946, Afghanistan's ambitious young king, Zahir Shah, hired a famed American heavy engineering firm, Morrison Knudsen, to build dams, irrigation canals, and a vast electrical grid across southern Afghanistan. At the time, palace coffers brimmed with profits from the sale of one of the country's few exports: Karakul fur from fat-tailed sheep. With European Karakul supplies cut off by World War II, the value of Afghan Karakul had soared, and with it, Afghan confidence.

Hubris filled the Boise, Idaho, headquarters of Morrison Knudsen as well. The firm embodied the growing industrial might and can-do ethos of post–World War II America. Its executives believed that the dams, canals, and roads they constructed around the globe continued the inevitable march of human progress. In 1954, *Time* magazine hailed the firm's cofounder Harry Morrison as "the man who has done more than anyone else to change the face of the earth." In the United States, the firm achieved its goals. In a forty-year span, it helped build the Hoover Dam, the Kennedy Space Center, and the Trans-Alaska Pipeline. But in Afghanistan, its project quickly went awry.

Afghan officials dismissed recommendations from Morrison Knudsen that the soil in Helmand be tested before constructing the irrigation canals. When water later flowed into desert fields, salt deposits in the soil killed crops. As costs spiraled, the Afghan government struggled to pay Morrison Knudsen. The high-stakes scheme flirted with collapse.

Fearing a loss of American prestige to the Soviet Union if the project failed, the U.S. Export-Import Bank began providing loans in the early 1950s. Eager to outdo the Soviets, American officials eventually promised to create an Afghanistan version of the Tennessee Valley Authority, the Depression-era hydroelectric system that spans five American states. The newly created Helmand Valley Authority would employ thousands of Afghan engineers and farmers and turn southern Afghanistan into the country's new breadbasket.

In the spring of 1960, the British historian Arnold J. Toynbee visited Helmand and discovered "a piece of America inserted into the Afghan landscape." Driving along miles of newly built canals, Toynbee felt as if he were traversing the southwestern United States, where American hubris seemed to have conquered nature. "The river that they are bleeding might be, not the Helmand, but the Colorado," Toynbee wrote in a memoir of his journey.

Laid out in a neat square grid, cold war Lashkar Gah was a sweltering, dust-covered town of fifteen thousand perched above the swirling brown waters of the Helmand River. Afghanistan's longest waterway, the Helmand sprouted green fields and orchards along its shores as it meandered through hundreds of miles of desert. The town had a four-lane, pine-tree-lined Main Street, a new hotel with a swimming pool and a tennis court, and southern Afghanistan's only coeducational high school. Downtown, a new movie theater played the latest Indian films. A few blocks away, American families ate hamburgers and watched Hollywood movies in a USAID guesthouse with a backyard cinema and patio.

The Americans prided themselves on being different from the British, but hints of colonialism emerged. Lucy Shook, a New Mexico housewife and devout Mormon, managed the USAID guesthouse in Lashkar Gah from 1965 to 1970. Young Afghan men wore bow ties, cooked food, and worked as servants. Shook called them "her boys." Educated Afghan engineers, doctors, and teachers from Kabul worked with the Americans on the project. Farmers, shopkeepers, and traders made up the remainder of the population.

The province and its massive development project even became the setting of a James Michener novel. After traveling through Afghanistan in the 1950s, Michener wrote *Caravans,* a 1963 yarn that described local Afghan disappointment with an expensive foreign aid project that failed to meet their expectations.

David Champagne, a Peace Corps worker from California who taught English in the local high school from 1968 to 1971, recalled a poor but peaceful community where Americans and Afghans alike never locked their doors. His wife, a fellow Peace Corps volunteer, worked as a nurse in the local hospital. They were "heady times," he later told me.

Champagne worked at an experimental school where Afghan and American teachers tried to infuse students—particularly girls— with a sense that they could achieve anything through hard work. Trying to combine "realism and optimism," he told young Afghans that long-term education and government reform could create prosperity.

In the end, the elaborate Afghan and American project irrigated only half of the acres promised. It consumed twice as much American and Afghan government funding as planned and took three times as long to complete. But its training programs produced hundreds of Afghan engineers and technicians with "American mindedness," according to Toynbee.

"Most of them have lived and worked and studied in the United States; some have married American wives," he wrote. "The new world that they are conjuring up out of the desert at the Helmand River's expense is to be an America-in-Asia."

Among the young Afghans who were transformed in the process was Fowzea Olomi. One of the first girls to attend the city's new coeducational school, she went on to become one of Helmand's first women to graduate from college. When I met her in 2004, Olomi remembered only a handful of words in English. But she could still tick off the names of her American teachers and recite verses of

"Twinkle, Twinkle, Little Star" and "Puff the Magic Dragon." After school, she played basketball with American children.

"It was a very good time," Olomi told me, eulogizing the functioning schools, clean streets, and tranquility of Lashkar Gah in the 1960s and 1970s. "I was very happy."

But her good fortune, like that of Lashkar Gah's, would be short-lived. Americans abandoned the city in the summer of 1979 as violence spread across the country just before the Soviet invasion. Twenty years of guerrilla and civil war ensued.

By the early 1990s, soldiers-turned-thieves roamed Lashkar Gah's streets, and warlords encouraged local farmers to grow opium poppies, the raw form of heroin. In 1994, residents welcomed the rise of the Taliban in Helmand's remote villages and applauded when thieves had their hands chopped off on a local soccer field. Crime plummeted.

For Olomi and other women, life fell apart. Her husband, who had gone to Russia to study medicine and resettled there, abandoned Olomi. In Lashkar Gah, Taliban religious police closed a girls' school she had opened to support herself. Olomi, who had chosen her husband at the age of twenty-five, watched helplessly as her daughter was forced by her husband's brothers to marry a cousin at thirteen.

Her hopes rose again in 2001, when American bombs drove the Taliban from power. Olomi dreamed of another American-backed renaissance.

"At that time, we really felt so happy," she said. "We felt that we were free now."

In June 2004, I drove into Lashkar Gah with Charles Grader and found a bustling town of a hundred thousand people filled with shops and open-air markets. The prosperity, though, was illusory.

The boom was largely fueled by Helmand's trade in opium poppy, the raw form of heroin, which had been spreading across the province since the fall of the Taliban. Throughout the trip, eight Afghan security guards hired by Grader's employer accompanied us for safety reasons.

In the center of town, the remains of Little America still stood. Afghans had erected eight-foot-high mud-brick walls around the one-story suburban tract homes the Americans had built during the cold war, a sign of differing Afghan and American notions of privacy. Rows of pine trees still lined some streets. And the headquarters of the Helmand Valley Authority—an impressive two-story office building—was in remarkably good shape. In some ways, Lashkar Gah reminded me of a small town in Texas, which bustled in the morning and grew still in stifling afternoon heat.

The province's governor, Sher Muhammad Akhundzada, was allegedly enmeshed in the opium trade, residents later told me, and enriching his own tribe at the expense of others. When I asked him about it, Akhundzada denied engaging in trafficking or victimizing other tribes. In the years to come, the drug trade and the corruption it spawned would act as a cancer in Helmand, creating dubious fortunes, deep inequality, and simmering anger at government corruption.

In a series of meetings with local officials during our 2004 trip, Grader promised to create public-works projects that would repair the province's American-built irrigation system, employ local farmers, and give them an alternative to poppy growing. As we crisscrossed the town that day, he defended the thirty-year cold war American project from critics who called it a costly boondoggle. Yes, the project had enormous cost overruns and failed to irrigate the acres promised, Grader said, but it trained thousands of Afghans.

"I feel so good about the education here," he said after meeting an Afghan engineer taught by Americans in the 1970s. "USAID trained a lot of people."

Grader was a marker of how the American approach to development had changed since the cold war. No longer a government worker, he was a private contractor paid $130,000 a year by Chemonics International, a for-profit consulting firm based in Washington. From Kabul, he managed a $130 million USAID contract to revitalize agriculture across southern Afghanistan and slow the exploding cultivation of opium poppy. The year before, Grader had spent six months in Iraq managing a $62 million USAID education reform contract for a Washington for-profit consulting firm named Creative Associates International.

Instead of USAID implementing projects itself, the agency doled out government aid money to private contractors, who then hired a cascading series of subcontractors to actually carry out the work. Chemonics was one of several dozen Washington-based contracting firms known as "Beltway bandits" established in response to the privatization of government services by the Reagan, Bush, and Clinton administrations. The owner of Chemonics, an Arizona businessman named Scott Spangler, worked at USAID as a political appointee during the George H. W. Bush administration. During the 1990s, he and his wife contributed $98,000 to political candidates, all Republicans. By 2004, 95 percent of the firm's $185 million in annual revenue came from USAID.

Under George W. Bush, the amount of money going to contractors rose by 70 percent. In theory, the use of contractors created competition between firms that saved taxpayers money, slowed the growth of the federal work force, and provided better services. Contractors could also be hired quickly, avoiding glacial federal government hiring procedures. And they could be let go as soon as a project was completed.

But Afghans loathed foreign contractors. They cited studies showing that 40 percent of foreign aid eventually returned to donor countries in the form of contractor profits. An Afghan engineer who worked for Grader said both Americans and Afghans were corrupt. Americans made their money through high overhead and expense rates, he said. Afghans made their money through old-fashioned kickbacks and bribes.

"For you, it's white-collar crime," he told me. "For us, it's blue-collar crime."

Lanky, with a thick shock of gray hair and a faded all-American look, Grader was an eclectic cold war throwback with renaissance flair. Perennially clad in brown bucks, he wore khaki pants and blue Brooks Brothers button-down shirts. The son of a postmaster and a housewife, he grew up in Marblehead, Massachusetts, a community north of Boston that the Graders had inhabited since the 1700s.

After graduating from high school, he went to sea as a sailor on a Liberian tanker. Later, he attended the Coast Guard Academy, earned a bachelor's degree from Boston University, studied at the London School of Economics, received a doctorate in economics from Tuft University's Fletcher School of Law and Diplomacy, and earned an MBA from the Massachusetts Institute of Technology.

His USAID career spanned the 1960s and 1970s, and Grader made his name as an advocate for reducing American staff at USAID missions and increasing the local staff. After retiring from USAID, Grader served as CEO of the world's largest bauxite mine in Guinea for five years, ran the senior executives program at MIT for a decade, and then returned to Afghanistan in 1996 as managing director of Afghanaid, a British NGO. His family had affectionately dubbed him "The Indiana Jones of Marblehead." A divorced father of two and lifelong vegetarian, Grader lived in a rented house in Kabul and spent his nights cooking cheese soufflés, listening to Italian opera, and reading Thucydides. He worried that America was in danger of following the path of ancient Athens, overextending itself and succumbing to Sparta.

Grader sometimes overextended in his own life. In 1997, he was nearly captured and killed by the Taliban while working with his Afghanaid team in northern Afghanistan. In 2003, airport customs officials arrested him in New Delhi after they found British colonial-era rifles from Afghanistan in his suitcase. Falsely accused of smuggling antiquities, he spent five weeks in a fetid Indian jail. When American diplomats came to visit Grader, they found him teaching microeconomics to other inmates.

After spending the night in Lashkar Gah, we made the long journey back to Kabul. During the drive, Grader grew pensive. American society had changed since the cold war, he told me. Companies were less loyal to workers. Government agencies were more politicized. Expediency was the norm.

"I'm frightened by what we're seeing," he told me. "I really feel the integrity is less."

Later I learned that Grader was right about USAID. The agency was a shell of its cold war self. Exaggerated accounts of American aid being poured down "foreign rat holes" prompted Congress to slash its budget. USAID's worldwide staff had shrunk from a high of seventeen thousand during the Vietnam War to three thousand in 2004. Following the 9/11 attacks, the agency's budget doubled, but it received virtually no additional staff to manage a torrent of spending. Overwhelmed USAID officials bundled contracts together, creating enormous contracts that could be implemented only by large contractors.

Grader said that when he ran USAID in Afghanistan in 1977, one hundred Americans managed roughly $250,000 in spending each. In 2004, sixty Americans managed roughly $80 million each.

Staffers struggled to design, put out to competitive bid, and monitor hurried and sprawling reconstruction projects.

For Grader and other USAID veterans, the post-2001 effort in Helmand was an anemic epilogue to an intrepid American cold war initiative. "Our policy is screwed up, and it's costing us dearly in time, treasure, and goodwill," he told me, warning that Afghans would quickly tire of foreigners. "It really bugs me how inept our government is operating."

At the time, I assumed Grader was exaggerating. Like generations before him, he saw youth as feckless and society in decline. Four months later, though, Chemonics fired Grader after only ten months on the job. Company officials said they could not comment on personnel decisions. Grader said he was forced out after he dared clash with USAID officials about the agency's programs.

Several months after visiting Little America with Grader, I returned to Helmand to learn more about the contractors leading the U.S. effort. My guide was a forty-year-old ex–U.S. Army paratrooper who asked to be identified by a pseudonym—Bob Williams—for safety reasons. Grader had hired Williams's small contracting firm as the subcontractor to carry out Chemonics' agricultural development work in Helmand.

An affable businessman with a soft spot for journalists, Williams agreed to give me a tour of his USAID-funded agricultural development projects in northern Helmand, one of the province's most dangerous areas. I was nervous. Williams relished the excitement.

As we sped across central Helmand's Dasht-e-Margo, or "Plain of Death," in a battered Toyota pickup truck, Williams casually chatted with me. Disdainful of the bulletproof vests worn by other contractors, Williams was dressed like a suburban American father on a Sunday afternoon. He wore baggy blue sweatpants, a loose white T-shirt, bright silver Nike sneakers, and a baseball cap from "Ritchie Bros. Auctioneers," a Fort Worth, Texas, firm that sold used construction equipment.

The vista outside our windshield was otherworldly. Instead of driving down a road, we followed a worn set of tire tracks across a gravel-strewn desert. The earth seemed eternally flat, with heat waves shimmering on the horizon. There were no trees, plants, or other signs of life. Everything was a variant of the color brown. Behind us, two of Williams's Afghan employees drove their own pickup truck as backup.

So much chalklike dust seeped into the cab that my ballpoint pen stopped working. After we crossed an asphalt road, Williams made a breathless announcement.

"We're north of the highway," he said. "This is bad guys' land."

As we continued driving, Williams's life story emerged. He was an American adventurer like Grader, but of a different generation. The son of a lawyer and a stenographer, Williams grew up on the East Coast. After serving in the army and graduating from his state university, he married his college girlfriend and moved overseas.

After the 9/11 attacks, business exploded. By the time I met him in 2004, he had a $4 million operating budget, fifty employees, and a dozen American government and United Nations contracts to build roads, repair irrigation canals, and teach farming across southern Afghanistan. He specialized in completing projects in areas where other contractors dared not tread. Taking risks, he found, paid handsomely.

"This whole security thing has become a convenient thing for people to hide behind," he told me. "I'm no braver than anybody else."

In truth, the agricultural development program Williams implemented for Chemonics and USAID was a shadow of the earlier, thirty-year American effort. In the 1970s, a dozen Afghan extension agents worked in each district. In 2004, USAID—via Williams— employed only two per district.

Using private contractors should have created competition for USAID contracts. Instead, Taliban attacks in southern Afghanistan prompted many firms to decline to work in the area. With few competitors, Williams garnered windfall profits despite having little experience.

Williams had his critics. Chemonics officials praised his firm's agricultural work but called his construction work shoddy. One Chemonics official told me a Thai engineer Williams hired to implement a $700,000 USAID project to construct nineteen small irrigation dams was incompetent, did not understand English, and submitted an initial design that was "a crappy little drawing." Westerners who worked for nonprofit groups called Williams a war profiteer and said he hired away their best Afghan engineers.

"We've just been reinforcing the predatory practices," the American director of one nonprofit told me, referring to corruption among Afghans. "If [Williams] is doing shoddy work and pockets the money, it absolutely reinforces the way the system works."

When I later asked Williams about the criticisms, he dismissed them and said he stood by his firm's work.

As we made our way farther north, I grew increasingly nervous. There were no foreign troops in the area. Following the fall of the Taliban, the only American forces to deploy to Helmand were several dozen Special Forces soldiers. They built a base in the center of the province in 2002, hired several hundred Afghan gunmen to protect them, and focused solely on hunting Taliban and al-Qaeda remnants.

As Williams and I drove, the first of roughly two hundred California National Guardsmen were arriving in Helmand to create a

"Provincial Reconstruction Team." In theory, the unit would bring security to Helmand and coordinate construction. In truth, their arrival raised the total number of American forces in the sprawling province to a mere 350, a fraction of the number needed.

In the late afternoon, we arrived at our destination: a camp built by American engineers when they constructed the Kajaki Dam in 1953. USAID had awarded Williams a contract to renovate and modernize the camp for workers from the Louis Berger Group, an American engineering conglomerate. Under another USAID contract, Louis Berger would repair the dam's two turbines, which had received no major maintenance since the 1970s, and install a third turbine. The repairs and expansion, it was hoped, would increase electrical output by 60 to 70 percent.

As we entered the engineering camp, I was astonished. It was as if a replica of a 1950s-era American motel had been built in the mountains of southern Afghanistan. A cluster of small one-story bungalows provided lodging. A large restaurant served American-style meals. A dilapidated tennis court provided recreation.

"We could fill that baby up," Williams said, referring to the bone-dry swimming pool. "If we could get this going, damn, it would be nice. This must have been so cool," he added. "I just want to make this nice."

Early the next morning, we made our way to the dam itself. As he drove, Williams sipped Crystal Light iced tea, his favorite drink. For a five-minute drive, twenty-four Afghan security guards in six pickup trucks accompanied us. They were from another contracting firm, United States Protection and Investigations, a start-up security company run by a husband and wife from Houston. Instead of deploying the soldiers to secure contractors, the United States hired more contractors.

The dam was an 887-foot-wide, 320-foot-tall wall of earth that held back the swirling waters of the Helmand River. Behind it, an emerald reservoir shimmered brilliantly in the sunlight. During the cold war, American and Afghan engineers rode paddleboats and picnicked here with their families.

We walked into the dam's powerhouse and found ourselves in a time capsule. The turbines, office furniture, and bathroom fixtures had all been manufactured in the United States and shipped en masse to Helmand. The Golden Gate Switchboard Company of Napa Valley, California, built the electrical panel. Westinghouse manufactured the turbines. A Youngstown, Ohio, firm produced the gym lockers in the men's room. The building was a shrine to a bygone era of American manufacturing might.

For the last twenty years, Afghan technicians had jerry-rigged the turbines and somehow kept power flowing. Events since 2001 had puzzled them. Eighteen different groups of American officials, contractors, and engineers had visited the dam since then, they told us. Yet the Afghans were still waiting for promised repairs to begin. Williams and I had no answers. We made small talk, praised the Afghans for their work, and took a few souvenir photos. After a thirty-minute visit, we left as well.

Struggling to contain a raging insurgency in Iraq, U.S. troops handed over security in Helmand to British forces in 2006. When I returned to Helmand in the summer of 2007, 5,000 British troops patrolled the province, a fifteen-fold increase over the 350 National Guardsmen the United States had deployed.

Despite the earlier efforts of Grader and USAID, poppy growth continued to spread. Poverty, instability, and an epic five-year drought made the crop a talisman. Six years after the fall of the Taliban, the province produced more heroin than any country on earth, including Mexico, Colombia, and Burma.

On a blistering August afternoon, I met Williams in his base of operations in a former USAID house in Lashkar Gah. Williams rented out rooms to contractors and journalists for fifty dollars a night. A dozen Filipino construction workers employed by Williams lived in trailers in the backyard where Americans had held parties and watched Hollywood movies during the cold war.

A hand-painted mural on the living room wall was a vestige of the house's former life. It showed Afghan merchants selling their wares in a bazaar outside Lashkar Gah near Qala-e-Bost, a famed arch built by the Ghaznavid Empire in the eleventh century. The artist had signed her name in neat, cursive letters: "Janet Howard," she wrote, "June 1968."

When the Taliban took over Lashkar Gah in the 1990s, they declared the mural blasphemous. Under their interpretation of Islam, any portrayal of the human form is forbidden. Using white paint, they blotted out every human figure.

That afternoon, I joined Williams in the living room as he met the brother and son of a truck driver recently killed by the Taliban. His firm had agreed to pay the man's family one year of his salary as compensation. With a translator at his side, Williams greeted the Afghans warmly and tried to console them.

"We just want to say that when somebody gets killed on a project, it is a big tragedy for us," Williams said. "Your brother, your father, he worked with us for some time, so I got to know him personally. He was a hardworking man and always ready for any task."

Williams praised the driver for several more minutes. Then he asked if there had been any progress in identifying the killers.

"Thank you for your wishes," the brother replied formally, displaying little emotion. "We have no information about these people."

"Are the police not interested?" Williams asked.

"The area is not under the control of the police," the brother explained. "So they cannot do anything."

"The only thing we want to do—and it's a small thing—is offer some compensation, which we will do," Williams said. "I wish we could do more."

"We are also deeply hurt by this," he added. "It also deeply affected our morale."

The brother sat silently. Williams looked at the son of the dead driver, a wiry young boy who appeared to be twelve years old. "How about the little one," he asked. "Is he going to school?"

"Yes, he is in the sixth grade," the brother replied, adding that the boy was the eldest of seven children. "The others are smaller."

After exchanging more pleasantries, Williams departed and a member of his staff handed the Afghans an envelope. The man and boy politely thanked him and departed. I later learned that Williams paid the boy fifteen hundred dollars for the life of his father, the same amount the Afghan government paid the families of civilians killed in American air strikes.

The following day, I met Rory Donohoe, the new USAID representative in Helmand. Donohoe was, in fact, an independent contractor. The agency was so short on personnel that it hired contractors to monitor its contractors.

A twenty-nine-year-old Californian, Donohoe had an MBA from Georgetown and brimmed with ambition. His age and limited experience reflected a reality of the post-9/11 effort. USAID and other civilian agencies struggled to get seasoned, midcareer professionals to take posts in Afghanistan. Some agency veterans had children and were unwilling to risk their lives. Others went to Iraq, which was seen as more of a potential career builder.

Tall, with dark hair and a boyish face, Donohoe told me he viewed the free market as the answer to Helmand's ills. To curb poppy cultivation, he and USAID's new director of agriculture in Afghanistan, Loren Stoddard, were proposing sweeping new projects that would create markets for the export of legal crops.

One afternoon, Donohoe and Stoddard gave me a tour of Lashkar Gah's former Soviet airbase. They excitedly described a $3 million plan to clear mines from the base and turn it into an industrial park and airport.

Standing a few feet from rusting Soviet fuel tanks and ambulances, Donohoe described how pomegranates, a delicacy in Helmand for centuries, would be flown to emerging markets in India and Dubai. Marble would be cut and polished for construction. And a forty-year-old state-run cotton gin would be privatized and expanded.

"This could be the commercial heart of southern Afghanistan," Donohoe told me.

A few days later, Donohoe and Stoddard showed me a project to teach Afghan farmers how to grow chili peppers on contract for a company in Dubai. Stoddard, a burly thirty-eight-year-old former food broker from Provo, Utah, said he had launched a similar project in Guatemala where farmers sold chili peppers to Walmart. A USAID subcontractor had brought three white Zimbabwean farmers, who had been driven from their farms by supporters of President Robert Mugabe to help show the Afghans how to grow the peppers.

"These kinds of partnerships with private companies are what we want here," Donohoe said. "We'll let the market drive it."

From the start, though, security problems plagued the chili pepper effort. After local villagers sneaked into the chili pepper demonstration farm and stole produce, USAID hired watchmen.

Twenty-four hours a day, seven days a week, two dozen Afghan men with assault rifles staffed six wooden guard towers that ringed the farm, safeguarding the chili peppers.

"Some people would say that security is so bad that you can't do anything," Donohoe told me, "but we do it."

Asadullah Wafa, the province's new Afghan governor, told me that the American reconstruction effort was too small and "low quality."

"There is a proverb in Afghanistan," he said. "By one flower we cannot mark spring."

As their presence grew, the British vastly expanded the small American base in Lashkar Gah and built a one-story building that contractors called "The Hilton." British government civilians lived in a modern dormitory bedecked with photos of Queen Elizabeth, Monet prints, and wide-screen televisions. Soldiers built volleyball courts, gardens, and bars.

"There were too many people who were in Helmand that were not in Helmand," a British contractor who asked not to be named later told me. "They couldn't see beyond the walls that protected them."

British and American civilian officials dismissed the criticism. They said they ventured into remote parts of the province for weeks at a time, were repeatedly attacked by the Taliban, and narrowly survived several suicide bombings.

At night, I attended surreal cookouts in fortified Lashkar Gah compounds inhabited by British, Dutch, and South African contractors. White Zimbabweans and South Africans grilled boerewors sausage and downed gallons of alcohol. To me, they embodied the mix of sincerity, greed, and absurdity that marked the post-2001 effort. Some were desperate for work. Others were desperate for adrenaline.

At times, I felt pity for contractors saddled with Sisyphean tasks. In 2005, DynCorp International, an American defense contractor the State Department hired to train Afghan police, sent two retired American deputy sheriffs to train Helmand's three thousand police. One was a California native who had trained police in the Balkans. The other hailed from a small town in Wyoming. Before arriving in Helmand, he had never been east of the Mississippi River.

At other times, I was baffled by the schemes USAID approved. In 2005, a USAID administrator brought eleven Bolivian cobblestone road builders to Helmand to teach their craft to local people. Afghans, who had driven on asphalt roads for thirty years, were uninterested.

In general, the most effective foreign organization was the generously funded American military. Marine and army units mounted sprawling campaigns to both kill Taliban and create jobs. Highly trained young officers and soldiers were generally impressive.

"The war is good for contractors, for journalists, for generals," I scribbled in my notebook during one visit, well aware that I too profited professionally from Helmand. "The war is not good for the Afghan people. How do we create 'The Good War' again?"

Between trips to Helmand, I looked at the American aid effort in other parts of the country. Across Afghanistan, contractors dominated.

Of the five major contracts issued by USAID in Afghanistan, only one—health care—was given to a nonprofit group. Louis Berger, the construction firm repairing the Kajaki Dam, received by far the largest, a $275 million contract to build roads, schools, and health clinics. DynCorp won a $164 million contract for training police. BearingPoint, the global management consulting firm formerly known as KPMG Peat Marwick, received a $41 million contract to reform the finance ministry and the economy. Management Systems International, a Washington, DC, consulting firm, won a $15 million contract to improve governance. And Creative Associates International, another Washington, DC, firm, won a $16 million contract to reform education. Other American companies won contracts to reform Afghanistan's defense ministry and help the CIA gather intelligence.

The Americans employed by the contractors ran America's political and cultural gamut. The head of DynCorp's operations in Afghanistan was a deeply religious and patriotic retired brigadier general from Arkansas who said blessings before every meal. Now in his midsixties, Herb Lloyd was one of only three Americans to rise from private to general in the United States military. While growing up in Hope, Arkansas, he knew Bill Clinton as a "chubby little guy" a few years behind him in school. Clinton went on to Georgetown. Lloyd went on to Vietnam. Wounded during two tours with a Vietnamese parachute battalion, he served a third, winning two Silver Stars, seven Bronze Stars, and two Purple Hearts. He later commanded troops in the United States, Germany, and Korea, and taught at West Point.

Since retiring from the military, Lloyd had worked for DynCorp administering American government–funded police training programs in Bosnia, Nigeria, East Timor, and now Afghanistan. Bearish, balding, and divorced, Lloyd exuded the energy of a man half his age and carried an M4 assault rifle wherever he went. He had narrowly survived a 2004 car bombing that killed four Americans and three Afghans just outside DynCorp's Kabul compound. He leaned Republican, spoke openly of his faith in God, and had an enormous desire to help the downtrodden. One of his proudest achievements was his "chickadee dees"—forty-eight young Bosnians he had helped win college scholarships to study in the United States on the condition that they return home to help rebuild their country afterward. All but one of them kept their word.

An unflinching believer in his country, culture, and company, Lloyd was convinced that the sheer power of the American example would transform Afghanistan's bedraggled and corruption-riddled police force.

"Our motives are selfless. Human beings can sense that," he told me. "They can pick it up right quick."

Lloyd vowed to stay in Afghanistan until "the job is finished" and the "very culture" of the Afghan police had changed. Americans had no choice but to succeed in Afghanistan, he said. Otherwise, terrorism would again threaten the United States.

"There is no option other than victory," he said. "Otherwise, America as we know it will cease to exist."

Phyllis Cox represented another side of America. A Harvard-educated lawyer and the daughter of famed Watergate prosecutor Archibald Cox, she was hired by Management Systems International to implement a USAID program to modernize Afghanistan's courts. Blue-eyed, with an angular face and short gray hair, Cox grew up in Cambridge, Massachusetts, attended Harvard as an undergraduate, and received a master's degree in international relations from Tufts University.

Shying away from politics and pedigree, she moved to Colorado, got married, had two daughters, got a law degree from the University of Denver, and built a thriving legal practice of her own. After a divorce, she signed up for a short-term legal reform project in Cambodia in 1994. Captivated by the work, she moved to Liberia, Guyana, and Bangladesh to run legal reform projects there. In 2004, Management Systems International hired her to administer USAID's legal reform project in Afghanistan.

In a country where 85 percent of disputes were still settled by tribal law, progress was painfully slow. Religious conservatives dominated the country's Supreme Court. While gradually enacting some reforms, they used patronage, corruption, and deeply conservative legal rulings to try to hold the country together.

When Management Systems International's contract ended in 2005, another Washington, DC–based contractor, Checchi and Company Consulting, hired Cox to run a USAID-funded rule of law program. When her mother's health deteriorated in 2006, she returned to the United States. After her mother's death, she worked in Cambodia, Guyana, Liberia, and Haiti before returning to Afghanistan from 2009 to 2011 for more legal reform.

"This place gets in your blood," she said. "You have to see the process in small increments."

Cox was right. Though press coverage of Afghanistan was overwhelmingly bleak, there were pockets of progress in the country. While most Afghan ministries were corrupt, reform efforts in three ministries succeeded. In 2002, the Ministry of Health set a clear goal after the fall of the Taliban to build rural clinics across Afghanistan that would provide basic health care. With funding from USAID, the World Bank, and European donors, it hired foreign NGOs to run the Afghan government's health programs in different parts of the country. In 2010, a series of studies commissioned by USAID showed dramatic improvement. After eight years of consistent effort, the average life expectancy of Afghans increased from forty-two to sixty-two, the maternal mortality rate declined by two-thirds, infant mortality dropped by a third, and the percentage of women receiving medical care during pregnancy rose from 16 percent to 60 percent.

Critics pointed out that the survey was conducted in the safer parts of the country for security reasons, which skewed the results.

Still, the improvements—even if limited to more peaceful areas—were dramatic.

The Ministry of Rural Rehabilitation and Development took a similar approach. With funding from USAID, the World Bank, Japan, Canada, and Europe, the ministry created the National Solidarity Program, an Afghan-run $728 million initiative where twenty-nine thousand village councils across the country received small amounts of money to invest in the local project of their choice. Some villages built schools, others dug wells, and some constructed roads. Each village was responsible for maintaining and protecting its project after it was completed.

Afghanistan's third success story was the Ministry of Communications and Information Technology, which helped lead the country's explosive growth in mobile phone use. When the Taliban fell in 2001, Afghanistan's 30 million people had to leave the country to make a phone call. By 2012, 17 million Afghans—85 percent of the country's population—had access to mobile phones, and the sector accounted for 12 percent of Afghan government revenues. Across the country, 1 million Afghans were online. As many as a third of them used Facebook, according to one company's estimate.

Since 2002, the mobile phone sector had attracted more than $1.8 billion in investment from private investors, the World Bank, foreign donors, and the Afghan government. The cost of a SIM card dropped from $250 in 2003 to less than $1 in 2012. Along Afghanistan's highway network, more than sixteen hundred miles of fiber-optic cable had been dug, bringing affordable Internet access to Afghan homes for the first time. Internet service providers offered DSL packages in major cities. Other companies offered 3G and mobile GPRS connections.

In all three ministries, strong Afghan ministers crafted pragmatic, long-term strategies and patiently implemented them. Local involvement, realistic goals, and long-term commitments produced success. The question was how—or if—their success could be replicated.

In 2010, Little America became the epicenter of the Obama administration's troop surge. More than twenty-two thousand American marines—two hundred times the number of Americans deployed in 2001—arrived in the province. Roughly ten thousand British soldiers battled the Taliban as well.

Marjah, an obscure farming area outside Lashkar Gah built by American engineers in the 1960s, became the focus of a sweeping marine offensive. In 2010, the United States spent nearly $1.3 billion in the district, or $16,250 for each of its eighty thousand residents. The vast majority of the funding paid for American military operations.

Following the influx of thirty thousand foreign troops, security in Lashkar Gah and central Helmand vastly improved. The number of Americans assigned to training the Afghan army and police finally reached the levels American commanders had requested for years. The number of USAID officials in Helmand rose from one to eleven.

But a wave of Afghan civilian administrators promised by the government of Afghan President Hamid Karzai never appeared. Some effective local Afghan rulers emerged, but there were simply too few of them.

Donohoe, the young USAID contractor who oversaw other contractors in Helmand, became a USAID staffer, stayed in the province for three and a half years, and finally left Helmand in October 2010. Contractors complained about Donohue at times but respected him for spending so much time in the province. He was the longest-serving USAID field officer in Afghanistan. Most USAID officials—

and other civilians—rotated out of remote posts after twelve to eighteen months.

In a 2012 interview, Donohoe defended USAID's record in Helmand. He said only 1 percent of the agency's budget went to the cobblestone road and chili pepper projects. The agency completed the airport, doubled the electricity supply to Helmand, and reduced poppy production by roughly one-third. One of his biggest challenges, he said, was curbing an American tendency to do things themselves instead of relying on Afghans.

Eager to have concrete achievements during their one-year tours, American civilians and soldiers tended to implement projects themselves, Donohoe said. Afghan officials and firms often moved slowly and struggled with quality. By the time he left, he felt there had been a change in philosophy among U.S. officials.

"Everyone agreed that the only way for us to get out was for the Afghans to do things for themselves," Donohoe said. "The goal was to build an Afghan government that was capable of meeting the needs of its people."

During the cold war project in Helmand, he said, Afghans played a larger role in planning and decision making. And Donohoe found that the United States achieved more when it focused on a small number of modest goals over a longer period and worked closely with locals.

"Helmand is never going to be the Little America that was envisioned," he said. "But I do think Helmand is going to be okay."

If the United States continued to support Afghanistan, he added, the country would find its way.

"I think ultimately, the Afghans, they will figure this out," Donohoe told me. "They know what's going on better than we do."

Donohoe was right. Afghans often ran circles around Americans and other foreigners. But Karzai's failure to crack down on rampant corruption among Afghan officials proved disastrous. The greed of some contractors paled in comparison to that of many Afghan leaders.

Afghan governors appointed by Karzai profited from the drug trade in Helmand, seized land, and attacked rivals. With no strong institutions, merit system, or faith in the future, Afghans took whatever they could whenever they could for their families. Cynicism and graft ran rampant.

The idealistic Americans I came to know in Helmand met different fates. Grader, the cold warrior who served as my first guide in the province, never returned to Afghanistan. In 2010, he died in Marblehead after a brutal two-year battle with brain cancer.

Donohoe works for USAID in Peru. Lloyd returned to Arkansas. Cox moved back to Colorado. Williams, the contractor who took me to the dam, continues to work in Helmand. The Taliban or drug traffickers have killed seven of his Afghan employees since 2001.

In 2012, I met Williams in Washington. Under the Obama surge, business had initially boomed for him in Afghanistan. In 2011, Williams's firm had work in nineteen provinces. With U.S. forces preparing to leave, the number of provinces where he worked had now dwindled to seven. His company would never abandon Afghanistan, he vowed, and would continue to work there even if the Taliban took over.

The expansion of the Kajaki Dam that he spoke about so excitedly eight years earlier had still not been completed. In 2008, a five-day military operation involving two thousand British soldiers successfully moved a third turbine to the dam, and USAID hired a Chinese firm to install it. Yet Taliban attacks blocked the delivery of the nine hundred tons of cement needed to complete the job, and the Chinese firm abandoned the effort. Officials from USAID, which has spent $72 million on the stalled project since 2004, said work on the dam continues.

Missteps by contractors continue as well. A South African security guard who worked for the British government shot dead an Afghan colleague in 2009, was convicted of murder and sentenced to sixteen years in an Afghan prison. The *Washington Post* reported that former employees of Chemonics, which has received more than $430 million in USAID contracts since 2003, said their superiors kept their mouths shut about failing programs in order to keep contracts flowing. A spokeswoman for Chemonics said the company is now employee-owned and stands by its work in Afghanistan.

Louis Berger, the American engineering firm hired to repair the dam, paid a $65 million settlement after a whistle-blower exposed systematic overbilling of USAID. Company officials said the individuals involved were immediately fired, and the firm now has a new president, chief executive officer, and chief financial officer. And the husband and wife who ran the small Houston-based security firm that escorted us to the dam—USPI—pleaded guilty in 2009 to overbilling USAID by $3 million between 2004 and 2007.

U.S. troops stumbled as well. In January 2012, a video of four American marines urinating on the bodies of dead Taliban appeared on the Internet. Investigators later discovered it had been filmed in northern Helmand.

Williams loathed Karzai and other corrupt Afghans. But he also blamed American officials for failing to mount a serious effort until 2010 and instead relying on Afghan warlords to stabilize the country. In the process, they alienated the Afghan people.

"They see us coming and propping up these crooks," he said. "We do the same thing over and over."

Williams said he was ashamed of America's track record in Afghanistan.

"Our whole culture has changed since 2001," he told me. "What have we become?"

Looking back, we can see that Helmand acted as a mirror. Projects became more about Americans impressing their bosses back home than about creating lasting results on the ground for Afghans. American idealism—our great asset and flaw—faded. The name Little America took on a new meaning for me. It became a reference to a diminished America that had lost its way.

CHAPTER 2

Law and Disorder in Iraq

S ix weeks before American forces invaded Iraq in 2003, the Bush administration chose Jay Garner, a retired U.S. Army general, to be the American civilian administrator of post-Saddam Iraq. A blunt sixty-four-year-old Florida native who had led relief operations in northern Iraq after the first Gulf War, Garner began frantically pulling together a staff to manage a fractious nation the size of California.

Three weeks before the invasion, Garner met with National Security Adviser Condoleezza Rice and National Security Council officials to brief them on his plans. He and a team of experts from various civilian agencies said they believed a large contingent of American and European police officers would be needed to train a new Iraqi police force and prevent lawlessness. Garner unveiled an ambitious proposal to send five thousand American and foreign advisers to Iraq. Richard Mayer, a Justice Department police-training expert on his staff, had put together a detailed inch-and-a-half-thick plan that included organizational tables, budgets, and schedules.

The proposal was sweeping but not unprecedented. In Kosovo, a place one-tenth the size of Iraq, the United Nations had deployed forty-eight hundred foreign police officers to train locals and help deter crime. In Bosnia, two thousand international police officers had trained and monitored local forces.

In Mayer's analysis, two clear lessons had emerged from the Balkans. First, he believed that following a strategy he called "law and order first" was vital. If an effective police force and judicial system were not quickly created in Iraq, all other postwar reform and reconstruction efforts would stall. Second, Mayer believed that flooding local police stations with foreign trainers would help ensure that Iraqi police officers actually applied the training they received. The presence of foreigners also helped deter brutality, corruption, and infiltration by militias.

Garner and others on his staff warned administration officials that the Iraqi police, after decades of neglect and corruption, would collapse after the invasion. The police were "at the bottom of the security food chain," Garner recalled saying at the NSC meeting. "They didn't train. They didn't patrol."

Garner was not alone. In February, Robert M. Perito, a policing expert and a former official at the National Security Council and the State and Justice Departments, had made separately the same recommendation to Defense Department officials. Perito had called for six thousand American and foreign police officers to be dispatched across postwar Iraq.

But NSC officials reacted with skepticism to Garner's call for five thousand trainers. A vocal opponent was Frank Miller, the NSC official who would oversee the White House's effort to govern Iraq.

"He didn't think it was necessary," Garner said in a later interview. Rice, who was chairing the meeting, said the administration would revisit the issue after Saddam Hussein was removed from power. She then moved on to other issues.

"We settled for 'Don't make the decision not to do this yet,'" Garner recalled. "Let us get there and then make the decision on what was needed."

In truth, though, ideology was distorting administration policy. In a speech a month before the invasion, Defense Secretary Donald H. Rumsfeld said that international peacekeeping operations could create "a culture of dependence" and that a long-term foreign presence in a country "can be unnatural." In interviews, Miller and Douglas J. Feith, the Defense Department's undersecretary for policy, said their goal in post-Saddam Iraq was to minimize the American presence and empower Iraqis.

Feith insisted that his "strategic thought," as he later described it, was "that we are going to get into very big trouble in Iraq if we are viewed as our enemies would have us viewed, as imperialists, as heavy-handed and stealing their resources."

Rivalries and distrust between government agencies also skewed American prewar planning. Frank Miller, the skeptical NSC aide, said a CIA assessment led administration officials to believe that Iraq's police could maintain order. Doug Feith blamed the CIA report as well. He said agency analysts deemed Iraq's police professional, an appraisal that events proved "fundamentally wrong."

John E. McLaughlin, deputy CIA director from 2000 to 2004, said intelligence officials made it clear in prewar White House planning sessions that Iraq's police were troubled. He insisted that the CIA was not at fault.

"I left these meetings with a clear understanding that this police force was not one that we could rely on," McLaughlin said in a later interview. "I don't remember the agency, or intelligence more broadly, reassuring people about the police force."

Nine days before the invasion, President Bush rejected Garner's proposal and the recommendations of civilian experts. He approved guidelines that called for only a limited number of American police advisers. They would not have the power to enforce the law. That would be left to the Iraqi police.

Three weeks after American forces invaded Iraq, U.S. Army Lieutenant Colonel Robert Waltemeyer looked sternly at the thirty Iraqi community leaders gathered around him, put his hands on his hips, and read them the riot act. Forty-eight hours earlier, several hundred American Special Operations soldiers under Waltemeyer's command had driven Saddam Hussein's forces out of Mosul, the country's third-largest city and an ethnic and religious tinderbox.

"I came halfway around the world to protect your freedom," the frustrated colonel said. "You are the elder statesmen and wise men of this community and I need your help. We won the war and now need to win the peace."

Looting had erupted across the sprawling metropolis of 1.7 million people in northern Iraq, and unknown gunmen were firing on American forces. Waltemeyer—bald, stocky, and at times brusque— was trying to act like the new sheriff in town.

The local leaders, a cross section of Sunni Arabs, Kurds, Yazidis, and Assyrian Christians, listened politely to the American's speech but said nothing. As U.S. soldiers patrolled the streets in vehicles flying large American flags, some residents waved. Others spat at them.

In later conversations, local leaders and residents angrily complained that American forces had entered the city too slowly after Iraqi troops withdrew, and stood by as most ministries, colleges, and hospitals were looted. At the same time, clashes erupted between armed groups. Doctors said twenty-five to thirty people died in the first forty-eight hours of the American occupation. Over time, those numbers would spiral.

At the center of it all was Waltemeyer, a forty-two-year-old Special Forces colonel. From his base at the looted Mosul airport, Waltemeyer served as mayor, prosecutor, police chief, and public-works director in one. In public, he tried to convey the image of a take-no-prisoners strongman. In truth, he had only several hundred soldiers and no engineers, police, city managers, or other civilian experts to help him. Surrounded by an often hostile population, he and his troops were expected to somehow pacify and administer a city of dizzying ethnic and political complexity.

"Mosul has the promise to be a model community of a free democratic Iraq," he said at his first press conference. "But it ain't there yet."

As cities fell across Iraq, the same dynamic played out. Units of American troops rolled into towns and were confronted by angry locals who demanded that they police streets, repair downed electrical systems, and reopen schools. In Washington, Bush administration officials tried to play down the problem. Asked at a Pentagon press conference about the looting, Donald Rumsfeld gave an answer that became an infamous symbol of the administration's failure to properly prepare for governing post-Hussein Iraq.

"Freedom's untidy, and free people are free to make mistakes and commit crimes and do bad things," Rumsfeld said. "They're also free to live their lives and do wonderful things. And that's what's going to happen here."

It was also an example of an American tendency to focus on military force and ignore the vital role civilian efforts play. Military might alone is not enough to stabilize a country. Bush, Rumsfeld, and other senior officials ignored the warnings of career State Department officials, CIA analysts, and retired military officers that they would face chaos in Iraq. Instead, they were intent on quickly defeating Saddam Hussein's forces and avoiding Clinton administration–style "nation building." When they finally recognized that the United States had to mount a major effort to train Iraqi police, rebuild cities, and reopen schools, America's anemic civilian agencies were largely unable to carry it out. So were contractors.

In scores of communities across Iraq in the spring of 2003, scenes like the one I had witnessed in Mosul unfolded. Just as Garner's team had predicted, local police abandoned their posts en masse as government civil servants stopped coming to work across Iraq. Basic services disintegrated, and American military officers found themselves trying to repair municipal water systems and organize trash collection. Lawlessness, confusion, and uncertainty were rampant. In Baghdad, sixteen of twenty-three major government ministries were looted shells. Garner arrived with a team of twenty aides, toured the country, and tried to reassure Iraqis. But the postwar American plan to rule the country was in chaos.

After only three weeks on the job, Garner was fired by White House officials and replaced by L. Paul Bremer III, a former aide to Henry Kissinger. Bremer was even less prepared for Iraq than Garner. In a later interview, Bremer told me he had not participated in prewar planning and was never told of Garner's police training plan.

"I had only two weeks to get ready for the job," he recalled. "I don't remember being specifically briefed on the police."

When Bremer arrived in Baghdad on May 12, 2003, government offices were still burning. A full month after the fall of the city, looting continued. That night, Bremer gave his first speech to his staff.

"I put the very first priority on police and law and order," he recalled. "I said we should shoot the looters."

After Bremer's speech leaked to the press, American military officials promised him an additional four thousand military policemen in Baghdad. And a twenty-five-member Department of Justice assessment team arrived to draw up a plan to rebuild Iraq's police. They were daunted by what they found.

One team member, Gerald Burke, a fifty-seven-year-old retired Massachusetts State Police major, drove onto the grounds of the Baghdad police academy. Thousands of people—some, civilian crime victims in search of aid; others, police officers in search of orders—besieged a small group of American military policemen.

"We had people drive in with bodies lashed to the hood and lashed to the trunk," Burke recalled. "It was the only police facility that was open. People didn't know what to do."

The Justice Department team estimated that across the country 80 percent of Iraqi police had not returned to duty. Iraqis who had lived in a police state with virtually no street crime for twenty-five years were dismayed. They hailed Hussein's ouster but bitterly complained that the United States was not doing enough about spiraling crime.

In the face of soaring murder, kidnapping, and rape, Bush administration officials sent Bernard B. Kerik, the former New York City police commissioner, to Baghdad to lead the police training effort. Pentagon officials gave Kerik ten days to prepare for the job and little guidance.

With no experience in Iraq or overseas police training, Kerik said that one of the ways he prepared was by watching A&E documentaries on Saddam Hussein. He was never told of Garner's police training plan.

"Looking back, I really don't know what their plan was," Kerik said in a 2006 interview.

When Kerik arrived in Baghdad in mid-May, he found "nothing, absolutely nothing" in place. "Twelve guys on the ground plus me," he recalled. "That was the new Ministry of Interior."

Kerik put one member of his team in charge of training a four-thousand-officer unit to guard power plants and other utilities. A second aide was responsible for advising five hundred police commanders in Baghdad. A third was ordered to organize a border patrol for the entire country.

Kerik scrambled to reopen police academies and stations, screen thousands of Iraqis claiming to be policemen, and choose new police chiefs. Across Baghdad, American military policemen mounted joint patrols with Iraqis. All told, twenty-six hundred Americans tried to police a city of 7 million. New York, which has 8 million people, has thirty-four thousand police.

In rural areas, American military units launched their own impromptu police training programs that were completely separate from the civilian effort. Some lasted three weeks. Some lasted three days. Desperate for law and order, some American military officers declared local tribal leaders new police chiefs. In some cases, they welcomed repentant former supporters of Hussein back on the job.

Over the course of the summer of 2003, forty thousand Iraqi police officers returned to duty nationwide, and thirty-five police stations in Baghdad reopened. The numbers were promising but corruption was rampant. Insurgents and former criminals posed as policemen and infiltrated the force. And large parts of the population distrusted the former government officials Americans made police chiefs.

Fearing that long-term criminality and corruption would undermine any new Iraqi government, the twenty-five-member Justice Department assessment team drafted a plan to train a fifty-thousand- to eighty-thousand-member Iraqi police force. At first, members of the team suggested that Iraqi police recruits receive six months of training, the amount of time the trainers in Kosovo had settled on. Kerik said he "started laughing," and calculated that it would take nine years to train the force. The team reduced academy training to sixteen weeks, and eventually eight weeks. Later, a State Department audit found that some Iraqi recruits actually received the equivalent of four weeks of training.

"If you took all of the post–cold war conflicts from the 1990s and combined them together, it would not equal what you're up against in Iraq," recalled Carr Trevillian, the leader of the Justice Department team. "Even if it were a benign environment."

To make up for the shortened classes, Trevillian proposed a sweeping field-training program similar to the one Garner had outlined before the war. The team calculated that more than twenty thousand advisers would be needed to create the same ratio of police trainers to recruits in Iraq as existed in Kosovo. Deeming that figure unrealistic, they proposed embedding sixty-six hundred American and foreign trainers in police stations across the country to train Iraqis and, if necessary, enforce the law.

Officials from the State Department said they knew where to get the trainers: DynCorp. Like USAID, the State Department had gradually become dependent on the use of contractors over the course of a series of postwar interventions in the 1990s.

DynCorp's rise from a little-known Texas-based aviation maintenance company to an indispensable wing of the State Department began in 1994. On the eve of the American invasion of Haiti, officials in an obscure State Department office known as the Bureau of International Narcotics and Law Enforcement Affairs, or INL, received an urgent request. The administration needed forty-five American police officers to help secure the Caribbean nation after

American forces toppled military dictator Raoul Cedras and reinstalled President Jean-Bertrand Aristide.

INL officials contacted DynCorp, which already had a $30 million contract from the bureau to operate counternarcotics flights in Latin America. Impressed with the company's aviation work, INL awarded DynCorp a small contract to recruit, hire, and deploy the forty-five American police officers to Haiti. State Department officials viewed the hiring of DynCorp as an interim measure; DynCorp saw it as a business opportunity.

"We always saw it as a growth area because of the conflicts in the world," Stephen Cannon, a former DynCorp executive, told me.

Cannon was right. Throughout the 1990s, the government money kept flowing. A few months after winning the police trainer contract, DynCorp won a contract from the Bureau of Diplomatic Security to guard American diplomats in Haiti. When the United States intervened in Bosnia in 1996 and Kosovo in 1999, more money followed. All told, the State Department issued more than $250 million in police training and diplomatic security contracts to DynCorp for work in Haiti, Bosnia, and Kosovo.

After the 9/11 attacks, DynCorp's government contracts exploded. Between 2001 and 2011, the firm received $7.4 billion in contracts from the State Department and Pentagon in Afghanistan and Iraq. It became the third-largest American contractor in the two wars, behind only the massive oil and defense conglomerate Halliburton and a Kuwaiti-based firm, Agility, which provided food to American troops in Iraq.

While the Bush administration had largely ignored the need for police in Iraq, DynCorp had banked on it. After the invasion, the company posted help-wanted ads online and compiled a list of 1,150 active and retired American police officers who were interested in serving in Iraq. Under pressure for immediate results, the Justice Department team agreed that DynCorp should recruit the 6,600 trainers. On June 2, Bremer approved the plan.

The trainers, though, never materialized. Over the next six months, just fifty police advisers arrived in Iraq, even as the intensifying insurgency was presenting a much more lethal set of problems. Bremer, National Security Council staffers, and State Department officials all blamed one another for the problem.

"We and DynCorp were ready to go by June," a senior State Department official later told me. "But no money was provided for this purpose."

Miller, the National Security Council staffer who coordinated the postwar effort, said he was never told about the shortage of money. Miller said Bremer never made the need for field trainers a major issue. And DynCorp, meanwhile, waited.

"If at any point Bremer had said, 'I just saw a report and I need sixty-six hundred,' that would have made this a front-burner issue," Miller told me. "I don't recall that as an issue."

Bremer insisted that he pushed for more trainers throughout the summer of 2003. Over and over he was told that DynCorp was unable to find Americans and that no foreign countries were willing to send large numbers of police trainers.

"DynCorp was not producing anybody," Bremer said. "We were doing the best we could with what we had."

In interviews, DynCorp officials said they responded to all the requests they received from the government.

Frustrated by their inability to get enough manpower, Bremer and his staff cut the target number of trainers nearly in half, from 6,600 to 3,500. By September, they cut the number to 1,500. Finally, as 2003 came to a close, the State Department opened a sprawling training center in Jordan that would train 25,000 police recruits in the next twelve months. But once they went to their posts there would be few foreign field trainers to monitor them.

As the effort stumbled and shrank, no American officials publicly sounded the alarm about the situation. After spending only three and a half months in Iraq, Kerik returned to the United States. In early October, he praised the Iraqi police during a news conference with President Bush on the South Lawn of the White House.

"They have made tremendous progress," Kerik said. "The police are working."

Four years later, Kerik was indicted on federal tax evasion and fraud charges. He pleaded guilty and was sentenced to a four-year term in a federal prison in Maryland. The former leader of the American police training effort in Iraq is scheduled for release in October 2013.

After Kerik's departure from Iraq in the fall of 2003, infighting between American military and civilian officials involved in police training grew. American military officials announced that their training programs had produced fifty-four thousand police officers around the country. They said American soldiers would train another thirty thousand police in the next thirty days.

Civilian officials privately scoffed at the numbers. They believed that only superficial training programs could churn out so many graduates. Bremer said he repeatedly warned in NSC meetings chaired by Rice and attended by cabinet secretaries that the quality of police training was poor and focused on producing high numbers.

"They were just pulling kids off the streets and handing them badges and AK-47s," Bremer said.

Across Baghdad and the country, the spiraling insurgent attacks and lawlessness drove down popular support for the American-led occupation.

"We were the government of Iraq, and the most fundamental role of any government is law and order," Bremer said. "The fact that we didn't crack down on it from the very beginning had sent a message to the Iraqis and the insurgents that we were not prepared to enforce law and order."

Burke, the retired Massachusetts State Police major, said he was impressed by the eagerness of Iraqi police officers to build a professional new force but appalled by the American effort.

"We had such a golden opportunity in the first few months," he said. "These people were so willing. Even the Sunni policemen wanted change."

By January 2004, Bremer himself viewed the field training program as impractical. American military officials did not have enough troops to guard civilian trainers posted in isolated police stations, particularly in the volatile Sunni Triangle.

In a final capitulation, Bremer and his staff backed a plan to reduce the number of DynCorp field trainers by two-thirds, from fifteen hundred to five hundred. The remaining funds would be used to intensively train senior Iraqi police officials.

In Washington, Secretary of State Colin Powell and his deputy, Richard Armitage, fought the reduction. They argued that the police trainers could still operate in safer areas outside the Sunni Triangle. In March 2004, they lost the battle in Washington. The field training of a new Iraqi police force—at this point some ninety thousand officers—was left to five hundred DynCorp contractors.

When the DynCorp trainers fanned out across Iraq in 2004, they were disappointed and shocked by what they found. As one DynCorp trainer put it, they had hoped to be "part of an emerging democracy, part of history." Instead, they found themselves completely overwhelmed—and undermanned—for the task they faced.

As Garner's team had predicted, Iraqi recruits were generally motivated but their skills were rudimentary. In Saddam's Iraq, resources were showered on the intelligence services and army, which were seen as more loyal. DynCorp trainers had to instruct Iraqis on the most basic elements of policing, from designing crime report forms to carrying out traffic stops.

Reed Schmidt, a police chief from Atwater, Minnesota, said he was trying to teach the police in the southern city of Najaf his two-officer method for pulling a driver over when Iraqi officers said they preferred their own method. The Iraqis told him how two police pickup trucks with seven officers each surrounded the suspect's car with fourteen guns. Schmidt realized that if any of the Iraqi police opened fire they would shoot one another.

"Aren't you worried about hitting another officer?" he asked.

"Sometimes that happens," the Iraqis replied, according to Schmidt.

In northern Iraq, Ann Vernatt, a sheriff's investigator from Eastpointe, Michigan, said she and five other trainers checked on fifty-five stations each month. The hour-long visits left her impressed by the officers' motivation but dismayed by the bleak conditions.

"They had rusted Kalashnikovs, which they cleaned with gasoline. Most of their weapons did not work. And they got paid very little," she said. "They'd sell their bullets to feed their families."

Other DynCorp employees said their greatest frustration was simply having too many police officers to train.

Jon Villanova, a North Carolina deputy sheriff, said he was promoted by DynCorp to manage other trainers in southern Iraq four months into his yearlong stint. Under the original plan drawn up by the Justice Department team, he would have commanded a battalion of at least five hundred trainers. What he got instead was a squad of forty men to train twenty thousand Iraqi policemen in four provinces. Villanova said he couldn't dream of giving the Iraqis the one-on-one mentoring American police cadets typically receive. In the end, his team struggled to visit their stations once a month.

"That hurt," he said. "You need a lot of time to develop relationships and rapport so they trust you and are receptive to what you are trying to teach them."

David Dobrotka, the top civilian overseeing the DynCorp workers, said security concerns prompted him to stop hiring advisers once the number reached five hundred. Attacks were so frequent that some trainers were unable to leave their camps.

"Early in the mission, five hundred were too many," Dobrotka said. "Some were just sitting."

At the same time, there were only two government employees and one contractor in Baghdad monitoring the performance of all five hundred DynCorp advisers spread across the country. Government auditors later accused DynCorp employees of selling ammunition earmarked for the Iraqi police. And they found that DynCorp failed to install proper fraud controls and that a subcontractor it hired stole $600,000 worth of fuel in 2003.

Richard Cashon, a DynCorp vice president, defended the company's performance. The employees involved in the fuel theft were fired, and the company reimbursed the $600,000 the government lost. He said the firm's only responsibility was to provide high-quality contractors. The design, administration, and monitoring of the police training program were the responsibility of the State Department.

"We are not judged on the success or failure of the program as they established it," Cashon said. "We are judged on our ability to provide qualified personnel."

* * *

Even as the police training effort in Iraq stumbled, DynCorp won more and more government contracts. Government workers eventually started to refer to DynCorp and other contracting firms as "body shops." Whenever the government needed personnel to do anything, from interrogating prisoners to performing housekeeping on a base, DynCorp and other firms hired experts in the required field and offered them to the government for a fee. Between 2002 and 2012, DynCorp provided translators to American troops in Iraq and Afghanistan, maintained helicopters the United States provided to Pakistan, trained police in Afghanistan and Iraq for the State Department, and won multibillion-dollar Pentagon contracts to build, supply, and maintain American military bases worldwide. After Afghan President Hamid Karzai narrowly survived an assassination attempt in Kandahar in September 2002, the State Department hired DynCorp to protect him. Within months, State Department and Afghan officials began to complain that the DynCorp guards were far too aggressive in their tactics. Their conduct alienated Afghan and European officials as well as Afghans. American officials evenutally stopped using DynCorp personnel to guard Karzai.

Investigators later found that so few firms were willing to work in Iraq and Afghanistan that DynCorp won some of its largest contracts with little competition. When DynCorp was not included in a final round of bidders for a new police training contract in 2009, the company filed a protest with the Government Accountability Office and won. Despite seven years of questionable performance, DynCorp won another police training contract worth up to $1 billion in December 2010.

In the end, DynCorp and other contractors had little responsibility for the actual outcome of U.S. government efforts but continued to profit enormously. Under DynCorp's "cost-plus" police training contracts, the company spent as much money as it deemed necessary to complete a project, and the government agreed to pay a set fee as a guaranteed profit.

In short, it was impossible for DynCorp to lose money.

A bipartisan panel Congress created in 2008—the Commission on Wartime Contracting in Iraq and Afghanistan—found that the cost-plus contracts created no incentive for contractors to reduce costs.

"Their company was not carrying any risk whatsoever," said Charles Tiefer, a member of the commission and a professor at the University of Baltimore School of Law. "They had the government's credit card in their pockets. It was guaranteed, a percent profit."

The spectacular returns caught the eye of traditional defense contractors and Wall Street. In 2003, Computer Sciences Corporation, a longtime defense contractor known by its acronym, CSC, purchased DynCorp for $914 million. Less than two years later, CSC split the company and sold its security and aviation divisions to Veritas Capital, a Wall Street venture capital firm, for $850 million. Two years later, Veritas took DynCorp public. And in 2010, Veritas sold DynCorp to a Wall Street private equity firm, Cerberus Capital Management, for $1 billion.

Officials from Veritas and Cerberus did not respond to interview requests. DynCorp officials said Cerberus had changed 90 percent of the firm's top management and improved performance. Former DynCorp employees told a different story. They said that midway through Veritas's six-year control of the company a new management team began cutting corners, reducing costs, and emphasizing profit over performance.

In truth, DynCorp's owners and executives took advantage of overwhelmed government agencies whose staffing had been cut by repeated administrations and congresses. High-priced contractors, it seemed, could solve any problem. In fact, they could not. But as the civilian American efforts in Iraq and Afghanistan faltered, the owners of DynCorp and other contracting firms grew rich.

The chairman of Veritas Capital, Robert B. McKeon, appears to be the American who made the single largest profit from the wars in Iraq and Afghanistan: $350 million from the purchase and sale of DynCorp. On September 10, 2012, McKeon committed suicide in his home in Darien, Connecticut, according to local police. A Veritas official who asked not to be named said the cause was personal and not work-related.

"Bob was an extraordinary person, a consummate professional, and a cherished friend and colleague," Veritas said in a statement. "We are all deeply saddened by this tragic loss and have his family in our thoughts."

The fifty-eight-year-old father of four was born in the Bronx and attended Fordham University and Harvard Business School. He established a fellowship at Harvard that helped military personnel attend business school. His suicide was a mystery and a tragedy.

CHAPTER 3

A Civilian Surge

Two days after taking the oath of office in January 2009, Barack Obama made a series of decisions that signaled a sweeping departure from the Bush administration's conduct of the war on terror. He signed two executive orders, one barring the use of harsh interrogation techniques on detainees, and the other ordering the closure of the Guantánamo Bay detention center. In a carefully staged Oval Office ceremony, a dozen retired American military officers stood behind Obama as he signed the order shuttering Guantánamo.

An event on the same day, January 22, 2009, drew less attention but would also have an immediate impact on the way the new administration battled the Taliban and al-Qaeda. Richard C. Holbrooke was sworn in as the Obama administration's special envoy to Afghanistan and Pakistan. For eight years, Holbrooke and other Democrats had assailed the Bush administration's strategies in the region. They said Bush relied too heavily on military force; mounted a paltry, contractor-dominated development effort; and made no serious diplomatic effort. Now Holbrooke vowed to implement a robust civilian surge.

But for the veteran diplomat, the next two years would be the most frustrating period in a storied diplomatic career that began in Vietnam and spanned five presidencies. On December 13, 2010, Holbrooke died of a ruptured aorta. Friends said he had worked himself to death.

In numerous ways, Holbrooke corrected and expanded the tepid Bush administration civilian effort. The Obama administration increased civilian spending in Afghanistan by 50 percent, from $2.8 billion to $4.2 billion. The number of Americans deployed in the country nearly tripled, from 531 to approximately 1,300, with roughly 380 posted outside Kabul. Across the border in Pakistan, American civilian aid tripled to $1.5 billion a year and staffing doubled.

Holbrooke slowed the illicit flow of ammonium nitrate fertilizer—which insurgents used to make roadside bombs—from Pakistan to Afghanistan. He focused so intently on agriculture that Secretary of State Hillary Clinton dubbed him "Farmer Holbrooke." And he reversed the Bush administration policy of supporting the eradication of opium crops in southern Afghanistan. He and American military commanders believed the practice only increased support for the Taliban.

In an effort to reduce the role of contractors, he funneled more money through the Afghan government and tried to increase Afghan capacity to rule the country themselves. He personally reviewed every contract issued by the State Department and USAID in Afghanistan and Pakistan. For years, Holbrooke had been preparing to make sweeping changes. In 2006, Holbrooke toured Afghanistan with a nephew who worked for the UN. Visiting a police training camp run by DynCorp in western Afghanistan, he was appalled by the quality of the Afghan police and DynCorp's operations.

Each day, DynCorp trainers drove nearly one hundred miles to the camp in large four-by-four trucks. Holbrooke warned the contractors that if they continued to follow the same daily routine they would be targeted. Six months later, four of the trainers died in a roadside bomb attack.

He also felt that the Americans were asking the Afghan police to carry out impossible tasks. At one point during the tour, Holbrooke and his nephew, Mathieu Lefevre, drove through the desert with American-trained Afghan counternarcotics police. Four policemen had one pickup truck to patrol hundreds of miles of desert.

"It was impossible with the current resources to interdict the drug flow," Lefevre recalled. "He realized that there is no way they can seal the border."

But bureaucratic infighting and political realities stymied many of Holbrooke's plans. In the American embassy in Kabul, Karl Eikenberry, the new ambassador and initially a Holbrooke ally, fiercely resisted any action by Holbrooke to encroach on what he saw as the embassy's authority. In Washington, USAID officials deeply resented his review of their contracts. And White House, USAID, and Kabul embassy officials all complained that contracts and dozens of other documents languished on Holbrooke's desk for months waiting for his approval.

After Holbrooke's death, the civilian surge was widely viewed in the administration and the region as a failure, doomed by a lack of local partners, infighting inside the administration, and mistakes made by Holbrooke.

Holbrooke's experience showed that the difficulties the United States encountered in Afghanistan and Pakistan went far beyond the liberal belief that the Bush administration had been incompetent. The countries' challenges were so complicated—and the degree of difficulty in solving them so high—that they would confound the Obama administration as well. And if Afghanistan and Pakistan were vexing, so was Washington. Steps that seemed simple on paper—such as decreasing the use of contractors—proved enormously difficult in the face of our own decayed and dysfunctional civilian agencies.

Holbrooke's first step at the State Department was to assemble an all-star team of experts and aides. As he had throughout his career, he broke through bureaucratic protocol and hired people with little government experience.

On the night before his appointment was announced, he reached out to Vali Nasr, an Iranian American academic and expert on Pakistan. Three months later, on a shuttle flight from Washington to New York, he made an impromptu job offer to former UN official Rina Amiri, an Afghan American expert on Afghan politics.

He also hired from inside the government. After Steve Berk, an obscure U.S. Department of Agriculture official, sent Holbrooke an unsolicited e-mail detailing his experience working on agriculture in the country, Holbrooke made him a job offer. When Vikram Singh, a young aide to the undersecretary of defense for policy, Michèle Flournoy, impressed Holbrooke during a trip, he hired him as well.

While the offers may have seemed spontaneous, Holbrooke was trying to create a group that would limit bureaucratic infighting. When it was complete, his thirty-member team had ties to every government department and agency vital to the office's success: Defense, Treasury, Agriculture, Homeland Security, Justice, USAID, the FBI, and the Joint Staff, among others.

As he had been throughout his career, Holbrooke was aggressive, tireless, and dominating. The sixty-eight-year-old diplomat, best known for brokering the 1995 peace agreement that ended the war in Bosnia, was known as "the Bulldozer." But in his new post, he exhibited less of his famed imperiousness, and encouraged, challenged, and supported his staff, according to former aides.

Over the years, Holbrooke appeared to have mellowed. He worked grueling hours and pushed his staff hard, but his advisers said they relished the experience. Comparing his office to an Internet start-up, they praised the veteran diplomat for keeping the organization as flat as possible. All staff members had access to Holbrooke, they said, and he encouraged frank and honest policy discussions.

Amiri, the expert on Afghan politics, said Holbrooke insisted that she typically present the local perspective on events, not the Washington view. "He looked at me to give the Afghan lens, not simply the objective lens," Amiri said. "How Afghans would see things on the ground."

In a September 2009 *New Yorker* profile, Holbrooke described his method as "a form of democratic centralism."

"You want open airing of views and opinions and suggestions upward," he said, "but once the policy's decided you want rigorous, disciplined implementation of it."

His dizzying travel schedule was another abiding belief that dated to his Vietnam experience. For Holbrooke, intricate foreign policy problems could be understood only in the field. As a result, he traveled to Afghanistan and Pakistan once every two months. Throughout his career, Holbrooke had been frustrated by Washington's glacial pace and bureaucratic myopia. To his dismay, those forces seemed more powerful than ever.

In an effort to fight back, he promoted staffers who thought and acted outside the Washington box. One of them was Shamila Chaudhary. In February 2009, Chaudhary briefed Holbrooke on Pakistan, and he was impressed by her knowledge of the country's politics. That night, the twenty-nine-year-old Pakistani American received a phone call telling her to join Holbrooke at a meeting with Clinton the following morning. The call stunned her. A civil servant, she had never before been invited to such a high-level gathering.

In the meeting, Clinton and Holbrooke discussed the various political players in Pakistan. Clinton said the administration should engage Nawaz Sharif, the former prime minister of Pakistan, and asked if it was true that Sharif talked with the Taliban.

"I made a joke," Chaudhary recalled. "And said, 'Which Pakistani government hasn't talked to the Taliban?'"

Holbrooke gave Chaudhary a thumbs-up after the meeting, apparently happy she had pointed out the Pakistan government's close ties to the Taliban. She impressed Clinton as well. The following day, Chaudhary was told she was being promoted to the State Department Policy Planning Staff, a career boost for a young civil servant. In 2010, she was named director for Afghanistan and Pakistan at the National Security Council. Her meteoric rise was a dream come true for Chaudhary.

The daughter of Pakistani immigrants, she had grown up in Toledo, Ohio, graduated from the University of Toledo in 1999, and moved to Washington to get a master's degree in international relations from American University.

"I had always wanted to work for the government," she recalled. "My family was able to come to the U.S. and have a good life here."

But Chaudhary struggled to find government work. She applied for internships in different government agencies, including the State Department and USAID, but had no luck. In 1999, she won a David L. Boren national security fellowship. Created by Boren, a former U.S. senator from Oklahoma, the fellowship is designed to increase American expertise in countries that received little attention during the cold war. Chaudhary used her fellowship to study in Pakistan, returned to Washington, and could still not land a government position.

Exasperated and desperate to do some type of government work, Chaudhary took a step she had tried to avoid. She applied for a position with a Washington-area contractor. Immediately, she was hired as an intern by the Academy for Educational Development, a DC-based nonprofit that implemented contracts from U.S. government agencies and others in 150 countries.

Quickly promoted to a job as a research analyst, Chaudhary found that there was not enough work to go around at AED, but the firm always managed to have enough money to throw huge holiday parties.

For four years, she worked for AED as it implemented various USAID-funded democracy and governance projects abroad. In 2004, she was finally hired by the State Department.

AED, meanwhile, rode the post-9/11 spending blitz, winning sixty-five USAID contracts worth roughly $650 million, including contracts to overhaul higher education in Afghanistan and carry out disaster relief, infrastructure development, education, and agricultural services in Pakistan.

Auditors discovered systematic fraud by the company in both countries. In 2011, AED agreed to pay back the government $5 million to $15 million and gave up all of its USAID contracts. While technically a nonprofit, AED paid its executives vast salaries. In 2007, its president, Stephen Moseley, was paid $879,530 in compensation.

For Holbrooke, the way to stabilize Afghanistan and Pakistan was clear: negotiate with the Taliban. But current and former administration intelligence officials flatly dismissed the idea. In March

2009, Bruce Riedel—a former CIA official—submitted a review of American strategy in Afghanistan and Pakistan to President Obama. Riedel concluded that the Taliban was uninterested in negotiations and called for a "fully resourced counterinsurgency effort" to break the Taliban's momentum militarily. Privately, the American intelligence community presented an even harsher assessment. CIA officials told Obama that the unanimous and uncontested view of the American intelligence community was that the Taliban was closer than ever to al-Qaeda. They said peace talks would go nowhere.

Holbrooke questioned the CIA's findings and opposed the blanket dismissal of diplomacy. He did not believe that negotiations with the Taliban should be launched immediately, but was convinced that peace talks would eventually be needed to extricate American forces from the region. If the talks were to succeed, he argued, years of careful preparation would be needed.

"For him, the purpose of his office was to devise a grand diplomatic strategy to end this war," said Nasr, the former adviser to Holbrooke. "The problem was that there were no takers in the beginning."

First, he wanted to see the outcome of crucial August 2009 presidential elections in Afghanistan. Afghan President Hamid Karzai, or whoever beat him, would play a central role in any negotiations with the Taliban.

Holbrooke and other senior administration officials were skeptical of Karzai. At a February 2008 dinner in Kabul, Joe Biden grew so angry at the Afghan leader's repeated denials of corruption that the then senator threw down his napkin, told Karzai, "This dinner is over," and left the room.

A month later, in a March 2008 column for the *Washington Post*, Holbrooke criticized the Afghan leader for failing to arrest an infamous Afghan warlord, Abdul Rashid Dostum, after he attacked, brutalized, and nearly killed a rival commander in Kabul.

"The effect on Karzai's standing and reputation has been enormous," Holbrooke wrote. "Excuses were made, but none justified his open disregard for justice."

Obama, Biden, and other senior White House officials were determined to no longer "coddle" Karzai, as they believed the Bush administration had done. Soon after Obama took office, unnamed administration officials leaked stories saying Obama thought Karzai was unreliable and ineffective. James L. Jones, the national security adviser, eventually advised American officials to work around Karzai as much as possible and develop relationships with provincial governors. And in an even blunter signal, Obama canceled the weekly videoconferences that Bush had held with the Afghan leader.

Holbrooke, meanwhile, focused on Afghan presidential elections scheduled for August. He wanted serious candidates to run against Karzai before the outcome became a foregone conclusion. And he hoped for a large turnout to ensure that the results were credible.

"He rightly or wrongly bought into the idea that the election could be cathartic for Afghanistan," said Nasr. "That it would produce a better government."

But the Afghan leader enjoyed a roughly 70 percent approval rating among Afghans, twice the rate of his nearest political rival. Most important, Karzai still enjoyed strong support among his native Pashtuns, the country's largest ethnic group.

Holbrooke's advisers were split over Karzai. Critics of the Afghan leader said the United States should try to quietly force him out. Others argued that ruling Afghanistan was an impossible task and that removing Karzai was unwise. And still others believed that only one scenario could defeat the Afghan leader: the myriad groups opposed to Karzai had to unite behind a single opposition candidate who was a Pashtun. The Afghan opposition, though, remained deeply divided.

Holbrooke urged several prominent Afghan American Pashtuns to run for the presidency—including former U.S. ambassador to Afghanistan Zalmay Khalilzad. When word of the meetings had eventually gotten back to Karzai, the Afghan leader decided the Obama administration was trying to oust him. In truth, Obama and Secretary of State Clinton—as well as Holbrooke— endorsed a "level playing field" strategy in Afghanistan. American officials would support any candidate who wanted to run for president but did not try to rally support behind a single opposition leader.

The approach proved disastrous. Each opposition candidate claimed—and in some cases believed—he was Washington's chosen surrogate. In the end, thirty people ran for president, dividing the anti-Karzai vote.

"No one knew whom the United States was backing," said a former Holbrooke aide who had opposed the "level playing field" strategy. "The whole process was mucked up by a very confused U.S. approach to the elections." Altogether, the United States and its allies spent $400 million on the August 2009 elections.

Some of Holbrooke's aides would later admit that delaying the election for several months would have allowed the administration to develop a clearer strategy. The Obama White House was overwhelmed as it tried to pass a massive stimulus to bolster the free-falling American economy, enact sweeping health care reform, and close Guantánamo. Opposition from congressional Republicans also slowed the administration's ability to fill positions across the government.

In Kabul, meanwhile, conspiracy theories swirled. An American hand was thought to be behind every major development in the country. On election day, Karzai's supporters—convinced the United States was trying to oust him—engaged in widespread voter fraud. Cell phone camera videos showing Karzai supporters stamping ballot after ballot for the Afghan leader were broadcast worldwide.

The day after the election, Holbrooke and Eikenberry met with Karzai to discuss the race. When Holbrooke, the senior American envoy to the region, told Karzai that he had not won the required 50 percent of votes and a runoff was required, the Afghan leader angrily insisted that he had won more than 50 percent of the vote and no runoff was needed.

After the meeting, Karzai called the State Department operations center and demanded to speak with Obama or Clinton, according to former administration officials. Obama, on vacation in Martha's Vineyard, learned of the request and contacted Eikenberry. The two men agreed that neither Obama nor Clinton would speak to Karzai.

Two days later, Holbrooke, Eikenberry, and the American and NATO commander in Afghanistan, U.S. Lieutenant General Stanley McChrystal, had dinner with Karzai. Eikenberry explained that Obama and Clinton would not speak with the Afghan leader. Karzai viewed the move as hostile and evidence that the British and Americans were plotting against him.

Several days later, the BBC reported that an "explosive" confrontation and "dramatic bust-up" had occurred between Holbrooke and Karzai at the meetings. European officials who were sympathetic to Karzai and resented Holbrooke had leaked exaggerated accounts to the media. The story quickly went viral. Across Afghanistan and the Web, Holbrooke was portrayed as Karzai's American taskmaster. Subsequent stories speculated that Holbrooke was trying to force Karzai to accept an American-backed "CEO" to run the government.

Two weeks later, tensions flared again. Peter Galbraith, the deputy special representative of the UN mission in Kabul—and a Holbrooke ally—accused Kai Eide, a Norwegian diplomat and the head of the UN mission, of covering up Karzai's election fraud. Eide, in turn, accused Galbraith of promoting a plan to force Karzai from office.

Galbraith resigned in frustration, left Afghanistan, and later publicly accused Karzai of being a drug addict.

An incensed Karzai refused to receive Holbrooke, and Obama had to send Senator John Kerry, the head of the Senate Foreign Relations Committee, to Kabul to meet with him. After receiving direct appeals from Clinton and Kerry, Karzai agreed to a November runoff. Then his chief opponent dropped out of the race, declaring the election process fraudulent.

For Holbrooke and the new administration, the election was a debacle. Karzai had secured another five years in office and was convinced the Obama administration was his enemy.

"If you're going to put a gun to the king's head, you pull the trigger," a former State Department official later told me. "They tried to kill the king and failed."

On one level, the Obama administration had made the same mistake as the Bush administration. Disdainful of its predecessor, the Bush administration was determined to distance itself from Clinton-style "nation building." The Obama administration, in turn, was determined not to "coddle" Karzai, as they believed Bush had. In both administrations, partisanship skewed policy.

At the same time, Obama's aloofness and unwillingness to develop strong relationships with people outside his inner circle— from members of Congress to foreign leaders—handicapped the administration. Obama's and Clinton's refusal to take Karzai's phone call after the first round of the election was a mistake. In hindsight, Bush's policy of consistent contact with the Afghan leader created a stronger working relationship with Karzai. Whatever an administration thinks of a foreign leader in private, a respectful public relationship is always more productive, particularly in South Asia, a region where public loss of face is deeply humiliating.

Holbrooke had erred as well. "Holbrooke was extremely blunt with Karzai," said one former aide. "You cannot behave this way in Afghanistan. This is not the Balkans."

Holbrooke, though, was also a victim. In his meetings with Karzai after the election, he was simply following orders from Washington to deliver a tough message to the Afghan president. In the months ahead, the White House would complicate Holbrooke's effort to mount a renewed civilian effort as well.

At the end of August, General Stanley McChrystal, the top American general in Afghanistan, presented to the White House his assessment of the American war effort. In a bold step, he called for a forty-thousand-soldier American surge to carry out the military's new counterinsurgency strategy. McChrystal also called for the United States to improve the performance of Afghan officials across the country and "prioritize responsive and accountable governance."

To Holbrooke and his staff, the assessment set off red flags. Holbrooke's experience in Vietnam left him skeptical of overly optimistic military assessments. The son of a doctor, Holbrooke had never served in the military. His best friend while growing up in Scarsdale, New York, was David Rusk, son of the former secretary of state Dean Rusk. After graduating from Brown University in 1962, Holbrooke joined the Foreign Service, was sent to Vietnam, and worked as a USAID representative in a small village in the Mekong Delta.

Over a six-year period he held a series of posts that gave him an extraordinary view of America in Vietnam. He worked as staff assistant to U.S. Ambassadors Maxwell Taylor and Henry Cabot Lodge. At the Johnson White House, Holbrooke wrote one volume of the Pentagon Papers, the secret history of U.S. involvement in the war. In 1968, he was part of the U.S. delegation to the opening of the Paris peace talks with North Vietnam. At a 2009 conference on Vietnam, Holbrooke delivered a critique of the war that many interpreted as a veiled critique of U.S. policy in Afghanistan.

"We pursued a policy that would have denied Vietnam to the enemy only as long as our ground troops remained, but would not have left the Saigon government strong enough to survive on its own. When we send our young men and women overseas to fight for their country, we must be sure they're really fighting for our vital national security interests."

In Holbrooke's view, a central mistake the Bush administration made in Afghanistan was relying too heavily on the military to achieve its goals. Vietnam had shown him how troop escalations were seen as quick routes to victory in elusive conflicts.

Vietnam also left Holbrooke dubious of Washington's ability to properly plan, implement, and sustain a complex, long-term effort. Whatever challenges lay inside Afghanistan, getting the White House, Pentagon, CIA, State Department, and Congress to unite behind a multifaceted plan was next to impossible.

"One thing he definitely understood was the daunting complexity of Washington," said Nasr, Holbrooke's former aide. "He knew what the strength of the United States was. And he knew its weaknesses."

In a 1970 essay for *Foreign Policy* entitled "The Machine That Fails," a twenty-nine-year-old Holbrooke—who had just ended his work on Vietnam—warned of the cumbersome nature of the American foreign policy apparatus. He said multiple government agencies—as well as multiple bureaus within the State Department—pursued their own bureaucratic interests and projects.

"Over time, each agency has acquired certain 'pet projects' which its senior officials promote," Holbrooke wrote. "These are often carried out by one agency despite concern and even mid-level opposition from others."

Forty years later, the lack of coordination and cooperation between officials and agencies was even more acute, he told aides and friends. While American military commanders viewed the counter-insurgency strategy in Iraq as a model for Afghanistan, Holbrooke, Biden, and Eikenberry were deeply skeptical. They argued that internal political dynamics in Iraq—not the American surge—prompted the sharp reduction in bloodshed there.

The debate came to the fore during ten National Security Council meetings Obama held in the fall of 2009 to review American policy in Afghanistan and Pakistan. At the State Department, Holbrooke and his staff prepared for Clinton a confidential paper on negotiating with the Taliban. Given the Taliban's success on the battlefield in 2009, Holbrooke was skeptical about their willingness to make concessions, but he thought talks could be an option in the future.

"He wanted that to be well cooked," recalled a second former aide who asked not to be named. "He wanted to make sure it was ready before he presented it."

Instead of backing Holbrooke's call for negotiations, Clinton dismissed it. She discussed the issue in private meetings with Obama and Robert Gates, the secretary of defense, but never raised talks in the National Security Council meetings. In late October, she told Obama that she supported McChrystal's request for forty thousand troops. Holbrooke agreed that more military pressure needed to be placed on the Taliban, but believed a diplomatic initiative had to be launched as well.

"In Holbrooke's mind, military pressure was key to any political effort," said the second former senior aide. "The problem was increasing the military effort in the absence of a clear political strategy."

On December 1, 2009, Obama announced a thirty-thousand-soldier surge in Afghanistan but said it would end in eighteen months. Politically, the president tried to strike a middle ground. Increasing the U.S. military presence helped him fend off Republican attacks that he was weak on defense. At the same time, putting an eighteen-month deadline on the surge appealed to Obama's liberal, antiwar base.

In Afghanistan and Pakistan, the deadline played out badly. Many Afghans argued that it encouraged the Taliban. The deadline meant that insurgents did not have to fight or engage in serious negotiations. They had to simply wait out the surge.

In Afghanistan's presidential palace, though, the White House's decision was interpreted differently. White House officials hoped that a time-limited surge would pressure Karzai to improve his own performance. But Karzai dismissed the deadline as posturing and remained convinced that the United States wanted to keep troops in the region to counter Iran, China, and Russia. Holbrooke declined to comment publicly but was privately dismayed by the lack of a diplomatic strategy.

For civilian agencies, the biggest problem with the surge was its size and time frame. Obama's time limit demanded immediate results. U.S. reconstruction spending ballooned to $4.1 billion in the fall of 2009. In Kabul, USAID officials outlined enormous new projects. More than $750 million was budgeted for increased electricity production. More than $300 million was to be spent in a single year in Helmand and Kandahar to revive local agriculture and reduce poppy cultivation—with another $450 million for future agricultural projects.

USAID budgeted another $600 million to improve municipal governments, $475 million nationwide to help reconstruct areas in the wake of counterinsurgency operations, and $225 million was budgeted for clean water. Another $140 million was for an initiative to train Afghans to properly appraise land and avoid property disputes.

In Kabul, USAID officials carefully tracked their "burn rate"—how quickly they were spending the money. In mid-2010, USAID officials celebrated when the spending reached $340 million per month. The figure became a sign of progress and was mentioned repeatedly in internal meetings.

The vast spending alarmed USAID representatives in the field, but the short time of the surge intensified the pressure for fast, visible results. In Nawa district in Helmand, USAID spent $25 million in a single year. The sum astonished the agency's local representative at the time, Scott Dempsey. The twenty-six-year-old former marine reservist turned aid worker calculated that the agency spent $312.50 for each of the remote district's eighty thousand residents.

Like Grader and Donohoe before him, Dempsey thought that spending the money over a longer period of time would be more effective.

"If that money could have been spread out with a long-term commitment," Dempsey said, "we would have been able to achieve long-term stability for Nawa, rather than good press for DC."

A final element that thwarted the surge was American infighting. To Holbrooke's surprise, he found himself engulfed in some of the most vicious bureaucratic infighting of his professional life. He never formed a close relationship with Obama and was never able to get a one-on-one meeting with the president.

Fairly or unfairly, Holbrooke's prominence in some ways made his job more difficult. His rivals in the White House and the State Department looked for the slightest indication of his famed imperiousness. White House aides attacked him, and on several occasions, Clinton blocked their efforts to have Holbrooke removed from his job.

Press coverage—an element that had helped him in the past—complicated his efforts. Inside the White House, seemingly positive press coverage hurt Holbrooke's standing. Aides to the president viewed the lengthy *New Yorker* profile as proof of Holbrooke's insatiable ego.

James Jones, the national security adviser, and Douglas Lute, the NSC official charged with overseeing Afghanistan, eventually went to bureaucratic war with Holbrooke. They denied him access to military planes when they did not want him traveling to the region. They limited the number of aides he could take on trips. And they held key meetings when Holbrooke was out of town.

As part of the effort to undermine Holbrooke's authority, he was excluded from the 2010 trip Obama made to Afghanistan after announcing the troop surge. White House officials knew that it would signify to Afghans that Holbrooke was not a major player in the administration. White House officials even plotted to have Holbrooke excluded from a 2010 Oval Office meeting between Karzai and Obama.

Lute, a retired general and Bush administration holdover who coordinated the Afghan war effort at the NSC, prepared talking points that would have had the American president tell the Afghan leader that the aides in the room had his "utmost support," according to press reports. Holbrooke, of course, would not be present. When Clinton heard about the meeting, she insisted that Holbrooke be included.

Friends of Holbrooke advised him to quit. Afghanistan was hopeless, they said, and he was wasting his time. Holbrooke insisted on staying. While he struggled in Afghanistan, he saw opportunity a few miles away.

CHAPTER 4

The Rise of the Drone

Three hundred miles to the west in Pakistan, Holbrooke was more effective. He stumbled at first but then made headway in a place few expected.

"He ended up having a much bigger impact in Pakistan," said Vali Nasr. "He wasn't competing with the military the way the military and the civilians do in Afghanistan. He [had] a grand strategy. He believed that we needed to stabilize the government and we needed to close the gap in trust that had developed for decades."

With fewer rival American officials and more room to maneuver, Holbrooke's frenetic, intensely personal style of diplomacy blossomed. After a series of early missteps, he formed close relationships with senior Pakistani civilian and military officials. And for a brief twelve-month period, he eased the deep distrust Pakistani officials felt toward the United States.

In Islamabad, he visited leaders every two to three months and held press conferences where he tried to address Pakistani concerns. When he was in New York, he barraged Pakistani officials with phone calls. In Washington, he took the Pakistani ambassador to the United States out for ice cream on Sundays.

The administration's first major initiative in Pakistan, though, went awry, illustrating another challenge American policy makers face: the U.S. Congress. Led by Senator John Kerry, Senator Richard Lugar, and Congressman Howard Berman, Congress passed a bill in October 2009 that tripled American civilian aid to Pakistan. But over the objections of Holbrooke and other senior administration officials, lawmakers put strict conditions on the aid. For Pakistan to receive it, the U.S. secretary of state had to certify every six months that the country's military was subordinate to its elected government. And the secretary also had to certify Pakistan was taking action against Taliban militants sheltering on its soil.

From the perspective of liberals in Washington, the bill was an effort to end a long history of American administrations—most recently that of George W. Bush—coddling the Pakistani military. Between 2001 and 2007, the United States provided Pakistan with roughly $10 billion in assistance. At least 70 percent of the funding went to the country's military.

At the same time, anger had simmered in Congress at growing evidence that Pakistan's military was sheltering Taliban militants they used as proxies in its fierce rivalry with India. The Pakistani army's policy of covertly supporting some militants appeared to be backfiring. To the alarm of Americans, members of the Taliban had turned against the Pakistani army and taken control of the scenic Swat Valley, which lies only one hundred miles northwest of Pakistan's capital. Members of Congress hoped the increased aid would show the United States' support for Pakistan's struggle against militancy, strengthen the civilian government of President Asif Ali Zardari, and signal to average Pakistanis that democracy, not the Taliban, created prosperity.

On paper, the bill was an attempt to create a more substantial and effective civilian aid program. But the Pakistani military deftly turned the conditions into an asset, not a threat. Pakistan's right-wing media—which has close ties to the military—declared the conditions an affront to Pakistan's sovereignty. Normally fractious opposition political parties issued a joint statement calling the conditions "humiliating." Instead of bolstering the civilian government of Pakistani President Zardari, the increased aid made Zardari look like an American stooge.

As the outcry in Pakistan grew, administration officials said they had asked Congress to remove the conditions from the bill but failed. Pakistanis simply did not believe them. As in other parts of the Middle East, the perception of the American government as a finely tuned, nefarious machine, not an unwieldy cacophony of viewpoints, was widespread in Pakistan. And the conditions reinforced a theme that existed in Afghanistan and Iraq as well. Measures that Americans considered well-meaning were seen as patronizing in the region. Americans focused obsessively on the power of Islamic extremism and often forgot that another force—nationalism—was even more powerful. If France had offered the United States $1.5 billion in aid with a list of conditions, Congress would have quickly rejected it.

As in Afghanistan, Holbrooke wanted to funnel as much American aid money as possible through the Pakistani government and increase its capacity. AID responded slowly, exasperating Holbrooke and his aides. He ordered USAID to immediately suspend its aid projects run by contractors and see if they could be administered by the state of Pakistan or local NGOs.

"AID is just slow, turgid, and bureaucratic, they cannot do the things we want," said a former aide of Holbrooke who spoke on condition of anonymity. "This frustrated Holbrooke to no end. Holbrooke would just light into them every week. 'Why are we not

doing big infrastructure?' 'Why are we not doing private investment?' 'Why are we not doing private sector development?'"

USAID officials and some American diplomats complained
that Holbrooke repeatedly shifted the focus of the American assistance, particularly in Pakistan. When the Taliban appeared strong,
USAID funding was directed to the border area of Pakistan, a Taliban stronghold. When the country's civilian government had a political crisis, USAID funds were redirected to areas that might
increase its popularity.

Officials at USAID said the government system was simply too
lumbering to carry out such rapid changes. Whenever projects were
changed, contracts had to be rescinded; contractors had to be fired;
and new plans, programs, and contracts had to be created. The frequent changes cost money and time.

Frustration grew so high that a senior economist at USAID
filed a dissent memo criticizing Holbrooke's review of contracts.
The economist, C. Stuart Callison, argued that Holbrooke's goals
were laudable but the Pakistani government and local NGOs lacked
the capacity to spend $1.5 billion a year responsibly. For such a
large program, U.S. contractors had to be used for an interim
period.

"On the one hand, [USAID] is expected to achieve high impact
counterinsurgency and broad-based economic development objectives as quickly as possible," Callison's memo said. "On the other
hand, it is asked to do this by working through national and local
government channels."

"These are all worthy goals," Callison continued. "However,
they are contradictory objectives without a reasonable period for the
latter."

By the end of 2009, American relations with Pakistan—and
Holbrooke's standing—had improved. In October 2009, Hillary

Clinton made her first trip to Pakistan as secretary of state. Mindful of the recent aid debacle and long-running Pakistani complaints against patronizing American officials, her office adopted a new approach.

After years of American diplomats holding brief, tightly scripted press conferences and taking few questions, Clinton answered questions from Pakistanis at public forums. She patiently listened to attacks on American foreign policy from students, editors, and others and tried to address their concerns. After the visit, Pakistanis praised her actions, which Holbrooke supported.

When epic floods engulfed Pakistan the following summer, Holbrooke personally coordinated American aid efforts. In many ways, it was Holbrooke at his best—overbearing, peripatetic, and passionate. From Islamabad, he drove the American government bureaucracy. He demanded that U.S. military helicopters be shifted from war fighting in Afghanistan to delivering relief supplies in Pakistan. He met with Pakistani officials and ordered USAID to respond to their requests quickly.

And he deftly managed the local media, not just the American media. On Pakistani television sets, American helicopters delivered food to stranded Pakistanis. In some cases, Holbrooke arrived in refugee camps before Pakistani officials did.

In many ways, Holbrooke's effort that summer in Pakistan showed how a revitalized civilian effort could achieve success. On a policy level, he focused on the practical. On a diplomatic level, he created respectful relationships with Pakistani officials. And on a public relations level, he improved the image of the United States.

In Pakistan and the United States, Holbrooke called for a more respectful long-term relationship between the two countries. Unlike his predecessors, he expressed interest in the long-term welfare of the Pakistani people. He stopped incessantly focusing on whether

Pakistan had responded to the latest U.S. demands in the war on terror.

And while publicly praising the Pakistanis, he was tough-minded in private. Holbrooke was fully aware that the Pakistani military was still supporting the Afghan Taliban as proxies against India and that some Pakistani generals were lying to his face. In a conversation with Holbrooke in 2010, I asked him why the United States did not cut its $1 billion a year in military aid to the Pakistan army. He said cutting aid was "off the table" because it would only increase distrust of the United States.

"This cannot be a transactional relationship," he told me. "We have to create a long-term relationship."

Holbrooke's other major diplomatic effort in the region—negotiations with the Taliban—also quietly gained traction. Despite the objections of General David Petraeus and other American military commanders, the White House privately agreed in January 2010 that an Afghan-led reconciliation process with the Taliban should be part of the U.S. strategy in the region. Four months later, Obama and Clinton told Karzai during a May visit to Washington that the United States supported his negotiation efforts. And on November 28, 2010, American officials and Taliban representatives secretly met for the first time since 2001. With German and Qatari officials acting as mediators, they held introductory talks in a village outside Munich.

Two weeks later, Holbrooke died. Within months, short American time frames and the White House's embrace of a new weapon in the war on terror would gut the civilian surge in both countries.

Six weeks after Holbrooke's death, Raymond Allen Davis, a thirty-five-year-old American, parked his white Honda Civic in front of an ATM machine in the busy eastern Pakistani city of Lahore. Stepping out of his car, Davis walked to the ATM, withdrew some cash, and got back into his car. Inside his vehicle was a Glock handgun, an infrared light, a portable telescope, GPS equipment, two cell phones, a satellite phone, dozens of bullets, multiple ATM and military ID cards, and a camera.

Several minutes later, Davis stopped at a traffic light and two Pakistani men on a motorcycle pulled up alongside his car. Both carried pistols. What happened next is disputed. According to Davis, one of the Pakistani men brandished a pistol. Fearing he was about to be robbed, Davis picked up his Glock and shot both men dead. Witnesses said Davis shot both men in the back, got out of his car, and tried to take pictures of the dead men with his cell phone. He also apparently called for help.

Moments after the shooting, a Toyota Land Cruiser with fake registration plates carrying American men sped out of the driveway of the house where Davis lived in Lahore. Roaring down the street, the Land Cruiser tried to reach Davis but got caught in a traffic jam. The driver jumped the median, drove into oncoming traffic, and collided head-on with a Pakistani man on a motorcycle, killing him.

The Land Cruiser fled the scene and sped toward the American consulate in Lahore. During the drive, the Americans hurled various objects out the window, according to Pakistani police. A baton, scissors, several batteries, gloves, a compass with a knife, a black mask, a piece of cloth bearing an American flag, and four magazines containing one hundred handgun bullets were later found on the road.

The Land Cruiser made it to the American consulate. But two Pakistani policemen apprehended Davis, who had tried to flee as well.

Pakistani officials jailed Davis, charged him with double murder, and demanded that American officials hand over for questioning the four men in the Land Cruiser. American officials said the four had already left the country. They insisted Davis was a security official at the American consulate in Lahore, was in Pakistan on a diplomatic visa, and enjoyed immunity from prosecution. Pakistani officials flatly disagreed.

Rumors swirled in the Pakistani press. Some reports said that Davis worked for Blackwater, whose shootings of civilians in Iraq had been reported and assailed. Some accounts said he worked for DynCorp, which had also won a contract from the State Department to provide security guards to the American embassy in Islamabad. Right-wing Pakistani commentators fumed on television about out-of-control American contractors killing innocent Pakistanis, Iraqis, and Afghans.

Three weeks after the shooting, the *Guardian* in London reported that Davis—who remained in jail—was a former American soldier working as a contractor for the CIA. The news confirmed conspiracy theories in Pakistan and the region about the sinister nature of all American activities abroad. The failure of American contracting in Iraq and Afghanistan now haunted the United States in Pakistan as well.

In the United States, the Davis case brought to light the CIA's exploding and poorly monitored use of contractors. The CIA—one of the most generously funded agencies in the federal government—relied on contractors to an extent never seen before. And, like other government agencies, it struggled to train and monitor contractors.

A 2010 investigation by the *Washington Post* found that roughly 30 percent of the people working for American intelligence agencies were contractors. Nine years after 9/11, contractors still played an enormous role.

"Private contractors working for the CIA have recruited spies in

Iraq, paid bribes for information in Afghanistan and protected CIA directors visiting world capitals," the *Post* reported. "Contractors have helped snatch a suspected extremist off the streets of Italy, interrogated detainees once held at secret prisons abroad and watched over defectors holed up in the Washington suburbs. At Langley headquarters, they analyze terrorist networks."

The *Post* found that in the aftermath of the 9/11 attacks the CIA had hired contractors as a way to quickly scale up the size of the organization. As elsewhere in the federal bureaucracy, hiring procedures were so byzantine that using contractors was the only way the CIA could rapidly increase its workforce.

Davis was not the first contractor to embarrass the agency. In 2006, a CIA contractor beat an Afghan detainee to death while questioning him in the northern province of Kandahar. The contractor, David Passaro, a former Army Ranger from Connecticut, was later tried in an American federal court and sentenced to eight years in prison.

In the world of espionage, Davis's actions were unforgivable. He had violated a core principle of spy craft—never draw attention to one's self. Officers in the CIA and other intelligence agencies are drilled over and over again to flee rather than get into a public confrontation.

After the *Guardian* disclosed Davis's work as a contractor, other news reports confirmed that Davis was part of a vast network of CIA personnel in Pakistan. Obama, skeptical of the American military surge in Afghanistan, had approved a clandestine surge in Pakistan.

When Barack Obama took office in 2009, "targeted killing" was a phrase rarely used in relation to his optimistic young presidency. The former constitutional law professor uttered the word *terror* only once in his inaugural address. Instead, he promised to use technology to "harness the sun and the winds and the soil to fuel our cars and run our factories."

Oddly, technology enabled Obama to become something few expected. In his first three and a half years in office, he approved more targeted killings—primarily through drone strikes—than any modern president. He also dramatically expanded the ability of the executive branch to secretly wage war. As the enormously costly military and civilian surges played out in Afghanistan, drones emerged as a comparatively cheap and politically risk-free alternative.

Between 2009 and 2012, Obama carried out at least 290 covert drone strikes, six times the 44 ordered by the Bush administration. After promising to make counterterrorism operations more transparent and rein in executive power, Obama has failed on both counts. His reliance on drones distorted American relations with Pakistan and other nations where they occurred, drove up anti-American sentiment, and created instability, not stability, over the long term.

After taking office in 2009, the new administration, just as it had done in Afghanistan, was eager to differentiate itself from the Bush White House in Pakistan. While speaking publicly of multilateralism, Obama adopted a get-tough, unilateral approach in Pakistan. He secretly authorized a stepped-up American intelligence effort, and the CIA vastly expanded its covert operations. At the same time, the agency was given more leeway in carrying out drone strikes in Pakistan's tribal areas.

The decision reflected Obama's personal belief and the influence of John Brennan, a former CIA official who was Obama's new senior counterterrorism adviser. To a far greater extent than the Bush White House, Obama and his top aides relied on the CIA for its analysis of Pakistan. As a result, preserving the agency's ability to carry out counterterrorism, or CT, operations in Pakistan became of paramount importance.

"The most important thing when it came to Pakistan was to be able to carry out drone strikes and nothing else," said Shamila Chaudhary, the young Pakistani American analyst who advised Holbrooke and Clinton and worked on the National Security Council. "The bilateral relationship was there solely to serve the CT approach."

Initially, the CIA was right. Increased drone strikes in the tribal areas eliminated senior al-Qaeda operatives in 2009. And in July 2010, Pakistanis working for the CIA pulled up behind a white Suzuki navigating the bustling city of Peshawar. The driver of the car was eventually tracked to a large compound in the city of Abbottabad. On May 2, 2011, American commandos killed Osama bin Laden there.

The American intelligence footprint, though, extended far beyond the hunt for Bin Laden. In the American embassy in Islamabad, CIA operatives and contractors outnumbered American diplomats and USAID workers. Davis was arrested in Lahore, a city where few people believed Bin Laden was hiding. At one point, the CIA tried to deploy dozens of operatives across Pakistan, according to Chaudhary. The agency also recruited large numbers of Pakistanis, including a doctor who pretended to be administering polio vaccines in Abbottabad in a failed effort to confirm that Bin Laden was hiding in the town. But the CIA's most controversial tactic was its stepped-up drone attacks.

Established by the Bush administration and Pakistani President Pervez Musharraf in 2004, the covert CIA drone program initially carried out only "personality" strikes against a preapproved list of senior al-Qaeda members. Pakistani officials were notified before many, but not all, attacks. Between 2004 and 2007, nine attacks were carried out in Pakistan, according to a compilation by the New America Foundation.

In 2008, the Bush administration authorized "signature" strikes in the tribal areas. Instead of basing attacks on intelligence regarding a specific "personality," CIA drone operators could carry out strikes based on the behavior of people on the ground. A drone strike could be launched if a group, for example, was seen crossing back and forth over the Afghanistan-Pakistan border. In its final year in office, the Bush administration carried out thirty-three drone strikes in total.

In 2009, under Obama, the total number of strikes nearly doubled to fifty-three. Former administration officials said the signature strikes, in particular, resulted in the killing of civilians. As the strikes escalated over the course of 2009, Pakistani public anger grew and the American ambassador in Pakistan, Anne W. Patterson, privately complained that she was not being consulted by the CIA before strikes were launched.

Dennis Blair, Obama's first director of national intelligence, also criticized the escalating number of strikes. Holbrooke privately proposed that control over drone strikes be shifted to the U.S. military, which would make them public, subject to strict legal reviews regarding the killing of civilians, and force the payment of compensation to the families of innocent victims. The CIA quickly killed the plan.

In 2010, the number of strikes more than doubled again, to 118. When Cameron Munter replaced Patterson as ambassador in Islamabad in October 2010, he objected even more vigorously to the attacks. On at least two occasions, CIA director Leon Panetta ignored Munter's protests and launched strikes in Pakistan. One occurred only hours after John Kerry, the head of the Senate Foreign Relations Committee, completed a visit to Islamabad.

After Davis's arrest in January 2011, the CIA paused drone strikes, apparently fearing for his safety. After weeks of public rancor, the CIA struck an agreement with Pakistan's intelligence service, the Directorate of Inter-Services Intelligence, or ISI. Pakistani intelligence operatives paid roughly $2.4 million to the families of Davis's three victims, and Davis was released on March 16. Nine month later, he was arrested in Colorado after getting into a fight with a man over a bagel shop parking spot.

The CIA—again over Munter's objections—immediately resumed drone strikes. The day after Davis was freed, the CIA carried out a signature drone strike that Pakistani officials said killed four Taliban fighters and thirty-eight civilians. Already incensed over the Davis case, Pakistan's army chief, General Ashfaq Parvez Kayani, issued an unusual public statement, saying a group of innocent civilians and local tribal elders had been "carelessly and callously targeted with complete disregard to human life."

U.S. intelligence officials dismissed the Pakistani complaints and insisted that twenty militants had perished. "There's every indication that this was a group of terrorists," one official said, "not a charity car wash in the Pakistani hinterlands."

Surprised by the vehemence of the official Pakistani reaction, the national security adviser, Tom Donilon, questioned whether the strikes were worthwhile. Critics inside and outside the U.S. government contended that a program that had begun as a carefully focused effort to kill senior al-Qaeda leaders had morphed into a bombing campaign against low-level Taliban fighters. Some outside analysts even argued that the administration had adopted a de facto "kill-not-capture" policy because it had been unable to close Guantánamo Bay and create a new detention system.

In April 2011, the director of Pakistan's intelligence service, Lieutenant General Ahmed Shuja Pasha, visited Washington in an effort to repair the relationship. Just after his visit, two more drone strikes occurred in the tribal areas, which Pasha took as a personal affront. In a rare concession, Panetta agreed to notify Pakistan's intelligence service before the United States carried out any strike that could kill more than twenty people.

In May 2011, after the Bin Laden raid sparked even greater anger in Pakistan, Donilon launched a White House review of how drone strikes were approved. During the review, though, the strikes continued. At the end of May, State Department officials were angered when Secretary of State Clinton's visit to Pakistan was followed by three missile strikes.

As Donilon's review progressed, an intense debate erupted inside the administration over the signature strikes. Admiral Mike Mullen, the chairman of the Joint Chiefs of Staff, believed they should be more selective. Gates warned that angry Pakistani officials could cut off supplies to U.S. troops in Afghanistan. Clinton warned that too many civilian casualties could strengthen opposition to Zardari.

The CIA countered that Taliban fighters were legitimate targets because they carried out cross-border attacks on U.S. forces. In June, Obama sided with the CIA. Panetta agreed that no drone strikes of any kind would be carried out when Pakistani officials visited Washington and that Clinton and Munter could object to proposed strikes. But Obama allowed the CIA director to retain final say.

Five months later, the administration faced the worst-case scenario that Mullen, Gates, and Clinton had tried to warn them about. In November, NATO airstrikes mistakenly killed twenty-four Pakistani soldiers on the Afghanistan-Pakistan border. A furious Kayani demanded an end to all U.S. drone strikes and blocked all NATO supplies to U.S. troops in Afghanistan from crossing

Pakistani territory. At the same time, popular opposition to Zardari soared.

After a nearly two-month lull that allowed militants to regroup, drone strikes resumed in the tribal areas in January 2012, but the frequency of the attacks slowed dramatically. As of November 2012, forty-three had occurred, half the number carried out during the same period in 2010.

Congress grew concerned about the accuracy of the strikes, and staffers in Senate and House intelligence committees began holding monthly meetings with CIA officials to review the attacks. But even with the CIA under more scrutiny, the strikes continued. The agency had won the battle inside the Obama White House.

Among the Pakistani population, the strikes have played out disastrously. In a 2012 Pew Research Center poll, 97 percent of Pakistani respondents who knew about the attacks said American drone strikes were a "bad thing," and 74 percent of Pakistanis saw the United States as an enemy, a 14-percentage-point rise from 2008. Other reports suggested that most Pakistanis dismissed American claims that 90 percent of the people killed by drone strikes were militants. They believed 90 percent were civilians.

Administration officials defended the strikes, saying they were popular with Pakistanis who lived in the tribal areas and had tired of brutal Taliban rule. And they contended that Pakistani government officials—while publicly criticizing the attacks—agreed in private that they helped combat militancy. Making the strikes more transparent would reduce public anger in other parts of Pakistan, U.S. officials conceded. But they said that some elements of the Pakistani government continued to request that the strikes remain covert.

While drones have battered al-Qaeda, they have not helped to stabilize Pakistan. The country's economy is dismal. Its military continues to shelter Taliban fighters it sees as proxies to thwart Indian encroachment in Afghanistan. And the percentage of Pakistanis supporting the use of the Pakistani army to fight extremists in the tribal areas—the key to eradicating militancy—dropped from a 53 percent majority in 2009 to 37 percent last year. Pakistan is more unstable today than it was when Obama took office.

In the end, drones are no substitute for the difficult civilian effort of helping local moderates stabilize Pakistan and marginalize militants. Missile strikes that kill members of al-Qaeda and its affiliates do not strengthen economies, curb corruption, or improve government services.

David Barno, a retired lieutenant general who commanded U.S. forces in Afghanistan from 2003 to 2005, said hunting down senior terrorists over and over again is not a long-term solution.

"How do you get beyond this attrition warfare?" he asked. "I don't think we've answered that question yet."

In the State Department and in Pakistan, Holbrooke's civilian surge slowly unraveled after his death. Clinton approached a variety of seasoned American diplomats about taking over Holbrooke's position but they all declined. Afghanistan and Pakistan were seen as doomed, and a quick route to derailing one's career. As in Helmand, serving in the region was not perceived as a one's patriotic duty; it was a carefully calibrated career step. Veteran diplomats wanted to know how the American effort in Afghanistan and Pakistan could serve their interests, not how they could serve the American effort.

Three months after Holbrooke's death, Marc Grossman, a retired career State Department official, was named Holbrooke's replacement. An able diplomat, Grossman had served as U.S. ambassador to Turkey and under secretary of state for political affairs. While Holbrooke had literally worked himself to death, Grossman took ninety minutes off each day for lunch and a workout, according to his aides. And in a trait that pleased White House officials, he cut off all contract with the media, stayed "in his lane," and focused solely on his area of responsibility.

When U.S.-Pakistani relations plummeted after the killing of Bin Laden, Grossman lacked the relationships and the mandate to ease Pakistani concerns. While Holbrooke had spent two years courting, cajoling, and delivering on promises to Pakistani officials, Grossman was starting fresh. Before the Bin Laden raid, he had visited Pakistan only twice. Arriving in Islamabad the day after the raid on a prearranged trip, he could do little more than listen to bitter complaints from Pakistani officials that their sovereignty had been violated.

Later, officials in the Punjab, Pakistan's largest province, rejected all American assistance, forcing USAID to reprogram the spending of $200 million.

In Washington, the White House marginalized Grossman as it had Holbrooke. When Obama made a secret trip to Afghanistan in May 2012 to sign a strategic agreement between the two countries, Grossman was not told of the trip beforehand.

And like Holbrooke, Grossman grew frustrated with USAID. The agency struggled to spend the $1.5 billion per year in civilian aid mandated by the 2009 Kerry-Lugar-Berman bill. Aides to Grossman said that the original goal of the bill was to mount large, visible projects—such as hydroelectric dams, canals, or roads—that would demonstrate America's commitment to the Pakistani people.

"They didn't believe in them," a former Holbrooke aide said, referring to large infrastructure projects. "They don't like them and they can't do them."

Development experts at USAID repeatedly refused to implement such projects. The agency's philosophy had changed since the days of the sprawling Helmand project. Training government workers and teachers and reforming health care were seen as effective development programs. Building dams, roads, and electricity plants were seen as bad development. USAID had become so politicized that it failed to follow orders. The former aide to Holbrooke described the mentality:

"We joined AID to do good development work in Latin America and Africa," he said. "We don't want to be part of your dirty war on terrorism."

While the American aid effort stalled, Pakistani business owners clamored for something else: access to American markets, private investment, and technology. After the 9/11 attacks, a central demand of Pakistani executives was that the U.S. Congress lift long-running tariffs on Pakistani textiles. The businessmen said they wanted trade, not aid, according to Chaudhary, the Pakistani American former State Department and White House official.

For years, the Bush administration tried in vain to get members of Congress to lift tariffs that protected their states' dying textile industries. Textiles imported from Pakistan into the United States, it was hoped, would create jobs and help stabilize the region. But members of Congress from both parties rebuffed the Bush White House. When Holbrooke tried, he failed as well. The inability of both administrations to get congressional support baffled Pakistani moderates.

"The families that own businesses, they say that to me all the time," Chaudhary said. "'We don't understand. There are so many of us that are ready and willing and pro-American.'"

Monis Rahman, a Pakistani high-tech entrepreneur, is one example. In the summer of 2012, Rahman was profiled by journalist Elmira Bayrasli in a magazine piece for the *World Policy Journal.*

Her piece—and future book—explores the challenges entrepreneurs face in the developing world. Rahman's rise illustrates how globalization and technology are changing some corners of Pakistan.

A talented student and the son of a UN diplomat, Rahman graduated from the University of Wisconsin at Madison with an engineering degree, Bayrasli wrote. Hired by Intel in the 1990s, he moved to Silicon Valley and worked on a team that developed a computing breakthrough: the Itanium 64-bit microprocessor chip.

"It was my dream job," Rahman told Bayrasli. "But once I got there, I realized that Intel wasn't enough."

With billions being poured into dot-com start-ups all around him, Rahman decided to quit his job and move back to Pakistan. He was determined to try to create the "next big thing." For him, it was creating Naseeb.com, Pakistan's first matchmaking site.

Before leaving, Rahman asked friends in Silicon Valley for advice, according to Bayrasli. He met with Reid Hoffman, the founder of LinkedIn, whose first start-up was an online dating service called SocialNet.

After talking with Rahman about how to make the site thrive, Hoffman asked if Rahman had found his start-up capital yet.

"I told him I didn't have the time," Rahman told Bayrasli.

Hoffman then picked up his phone and dialed a number.

"Joe? It's Reid," Rahman recalls Hoffman saying. "Listen, I'm with Monis Rahman, who's starting a SocialNet in Pakistan. I'm going in on it. I think you should too."

To Rahman's amazement, Hoffman had called Joe Krause, founder of Excite.com. Then he called Mark Pincus, who was working on Zynga at the time. The two men agreed to make $25,000 equity investments in Rahman's online dating service.

"Neither had seen any plans or PowerPoints on Naseeb.com," Rahman told Bayrasli.

He returned home elated but immediately encountered problems. When Rahman tried to find additional investors, he hit a brick wall. Despite the fact that international franchises like Pizza Hut, McDonald's, Kentucky Fried Chicken, and The Body Shop had proven enormously popular in Pakistan, investors were leery due to the country's instability.

"The main issue that we're seeing is we've got this huge perception challenge globally, and it is interfering with investments that are needed to fuel growth," Rahman told Bayrasli. "Many investors and businesses don't want to be linked in any way to what's happening here."

So Rahman started small. From a room in his parents' house in Lahore, he launched Naseeb.com in 2001. The space was so tight that when one of the eight staff had to use the bathroom, everyone had to stand up to get out of the way. Yet with only $150,000 in hand and expectations to succeed, Rahman didn't want to waste the equity investments he had raised before leaving Silicon Valley.

Nor did Rahman want to squander his connections there. He recognized that mentors and networks were critical to the life of any start-up. And both are scarce in Pakistan, Bayrasli wrote.

While there are established business families, there is no tradition of exchanging ideas or opening doors for others. There is no trust, Bayrasli wrote. Pakistani businesses fear that ideas and trade secrets will be stolen. With weak courts, there is little recourse. Rahman, though, was lucky. Unlike most Pakistani entrepreneurs, he knew he could find support in the Bay Area.

By mid-2005, Naseeb.com had grown to the point where Rahman had to expand his team. For that, he needed the best talent, so he put ads in the major newspapers, according to Bayrasli. Then he realized that was the wrong way to reach people who want to work for an online start-up.

"I built a site to post my own vacancies," he explained.

It got so much traffic that he turned it into a paid site, Rozee.pk, with a client list of 3,200 employers and more than 100 million job postings. Today it's Rahman's core business. After again battling perceptions that Pakistan was unstable, he received investment from Draper Fisher Jurvetson, a Silicon Valley firm with experience investing in emerging economies.

Rahman told Bayrasli he was doing more than making money. He was helping his country.

"It's more than just a service." he said. "I'm not just building a product. I'm trying to make people's lives better."

Rahman was not alone. The Acumen Fund, a New York–based charity, also managed to find a way to help Pakistan's poorest. Founded by a former Chase Manhattan banker, the nonprofit follows what it calls a "third way" of development.

Jacqueline Novogratz, the fund's head, argued that charity alone wasn't the answer because it too often failed to create long-term, self-sustaining solutions. At the same time, the market alone failed as well. Business ignored the abject poor because they did not represent a potential profit source. Novogratz embraced a concept she called "patient capital," which involves long-term investments in risky enterprises run by local businesses and nonprofit groups.

In Pakistan, the fund invested $14.9 million in organizations providing slum dwellers with affordable, legal housing; microfinance groups that try to help the poor raise their incomes to the point where they can buy health insurance; a group that helps farmers boost their profits by investing in livestock and drip irrigation systems; and a company building community clean water systems in major cities. Each project included follow-up by the firm's Pakistani partners, which included leading universities and companies.

In many ways, Acumen's approach was the opposite of the congressionally mandated spending of $1.5 billion a year under Kerry-Lugar-Berman. As of mid-2012, roughly $676 million of the $3 billion in civilian aid appropriated in Pakistan for 2010 and 2011 had been spent. After years of spending too little on the civilian effort in Pakistan, the administration tried to spend money too quickly.

Alicia Mollaun, an Australian researcher studying USAID programs in Pakistan, said Pakistanis perceive little impact from the American aid. "The Pakistanis say we don't know where it is going," she told me. "They say we don't know where it's being spent at all."

PART II
A Way Forward

CHAPTER 5

Where Islam and Democracy Meet, Uneasily

As the Obama administration effort in Afghanistan and Pakistan sputtered, the Arab Spring inspired and then alarmed Americans.

In an astonishing nine-month period in 2010 and 2011, street protests in Tunisia and Egypt and an armed rebellion in Libya forced the overthrow of three longtime Middle Eastern autocrats. Formerly all-powerful rulers in Yemen, Kuwait, Jordan, Oman, and Morocco made political concessions to the opposition as well.

In 2012, hard-line regimes fought back. Syrian President Bashar al-Assad's violent suppression of peaceful protests sparked a brutal civil war. The Sunni rulers of Bahrain crushed protests by the country's disenfranchised Shiite majority. And Saudi Arabia's ruling family tried to placate opponents with a multibillion-dollar increase in government benefits.

Finally, in the fall of 2012, instability spread to Turkey, a close American ally and a nation Obama administration officials viewed as a model for the region. After Turkey backed Syria's opposition, the two countries exchanged fire. As tensions mounted, Turkish observers complained about American passivity.

"We are now at a very critical juncture," Melih Asik, a columnist for the centrist newspaper *Milliyet* wrote in October 2012. "We are not only facing Syria, but Iran, Iraq, Russia, and China are behind it as well. Behind us, we have nothing but the provocative stance and empty promises of the U.S."

After decades of being dismissed as "the sick man of Europe," Turkey's economy, political system, and ambitions soared in the 2000s. By 2012, Turkey boasted a faster-growing economy than any European nation and a 40-million-strong middle class, roughly 60 percent of its population. For Obama administration officials, Turkey seemingly represented an alternative to the Middle East's three failed models of government: secular Arab dictatorship, authoritarian Islam, and American invasion. But Turkey's leader, Prime Minister Recep Tayyip Erdogan, displayed two contradictory sides.

Since taking office in 2002, Erdogan had overseen a near tripling of per capita income in Turkey; broken the Turkish military's decades-long grip on power; and declared that Islam, democracy, and capitalism were compatible. As part of Turkey's effort to join the European Union (EU), the conservative Islamist politician opened up the country's economy, overhauled its judiciary, and granted rights to women and minorities. He also completed a harsh International Monetary Fund loan and reform program and attracted massive investments from European and American corporations.

Erdogan also displayed a growing authoritarian streak. Over the past five years, Turkish prosecutors have jailed more than seven hundred people and accused them of plotting coups that would restore the military to power. Generals, members of parliament, owners of television stations, university officials, and journalists have all been arrested in what appears to be a campaign to silence dissent.

Critics of Erdogan—who was imprisoned for four months in 1999—say he is exacting revenge on those who oppressed him and his party in the past. In recent years, the Turkish leader has publicly assailed his critics and appeared increasingly intolerant of dissent. There are rising fears that Turkey will follow the examples of Russia and China: free-market growth combined with political repression.

Desperate for an ally—and a model—in the region, the Obama administration stayed largely silent about Erdogan's excesses. On one level, Turkey shows how free-market reforms, consumerism, and technological change can help transform a Middle Eastern country. On another, it shows how slow moving political reform in the region can be.

Culturally, Turkey has an impact in the region that the United States and other Western nations can never equal. One example is Turkish soap operas. Broadcast across the Middle East, they have taken the region by storm, empowering moderates and enraging conservatives.

Each week, in a state-of-the art Istanbul television studio, the Islamic world's version of America's culture war plays out in a television series called *Magnificent Century*. A dashing Turkish actor plays Suleiman the Magnificent, the Ottoman ruler who conquered vast swaths of the Middle East and Europe, granted basic rights to Christians and Jews, and promoted education, science, and art. Early episodes of the program portrayed a young Suleiman cavorting with scantily clad women in the palace harem and drinking wine. The sex was frequent.

After the show's January 2011 debut, Erdogan, along with a number of other Turkish conservatives, complained that it maligned a revered ruler known as "the lawgiver" whose military prowess and legal reforms placed the Ottomans at the zenith of their power. Erdogan called the series "an attempt to insult our past, to treat our history with disrespect and an effort to show our history in a negative light to the younger generations."

Critics hurled eggs at billboards advertising the program, protested outside the television station airing the show, and filed more than seventy thousand complaints with the Turkish government television agency. In response, the show's producers shortened kissing scenes and toned down other prurient elements.

In interviews, the show's producers defended the soap opera, saying it contained other themes. Its dominant character was a woman, the Ukrainian slave-turned-concubine who eventually became Suleiman's queen. And the story line showed members of different faiths coexisting.

Halit Ergenc, the actor who plays Suleiman, boasted in an interview in the spring of 2012 about the show's religious tolerance. "This is the most important thing of the Ottoman Empire that allowed one family to rule for centuries," he said. "Sharing the same land with different cultures and different religions and respecting their rights."

As of the fall of 2012, *Magnificent Century* was airing in forty-five countries and was one of the most popular shows in the Middle East. It was the latest of a series of Turkish television soap operas to find a huge audience there.

What may someday be known as the Islamic world's cultural revolution began in 2006. A Saudi-owned Arabic-language satellite television channel, MBC, bought the rights to an obscure Turkish soap opera named after its heroine, Gumus—"silver" in Turkish. In a classic rags-to-riches story, the series recounted the struggles of an impoverished young woman who marries into a wealthy family. Dubbed into colloquial Arabic, censored of its raciest scenes, and renamed *Noor*—"moon" in Arabic—the series was a phenomenal hit across the Middle East.

Unlike Western soap operas, it focused on an extended family, a strong tradition in Turkey and the region. In 2008, the show's final episode drew an estimated 85 million viewers over the age of fifteen, according to MBC. The audience included an estimated 50 million women, a figure that represented more than half the adult women in the Arab world.

Like *Magnificent Century, Noor* violated conservative cultural norms. Some Muslim characters drank wine with dinner and engaged in premarital sex. One character had an abortion. And in a subtle twist, the lead male character, Muhannad, was the show's moderate and modern hero.

A loving, attentive, and loyal husband, he supported his wife's career as a fashion designer and treated her as an equal. Their successful marriage—which combined traditional loyalty and modern independence—was both popular, particularly among women, and groundbreaking. Some Arabic-language newspapers reported that arguments and even divorces occurred in several countries as a result.

Turkish academics believe the programs have subtly changed cultural norms in the Middle East.

"Somehow, in those serials, you have a very balanced adjustment," Aydin Ugur, a professor of sociology at Istanbul Bilgi University, told me in an interview. "Women are modern, but they are not degenerate."

In Saudi Arabia, conservative Islamic clerics denounced *Noor.* They declared the show "wicked and evil" and a "secular Turkish assault on Saudi society." They forbade people from watching the program or attending prayer services in T-shirts that depicted the show's two stars. The head of a Saudi religious council said the owner of MBC should be tried and potentially executed for airing indecent material. Across the region, governments ignored him.

After *Noor*'s final episode, Turkish soap operas grew even more popular in the region and received glowing coverage from Arab and Western journalists. Beyond breaking cultural taboos, they displayed something else. In its soap operas, Turkey was modern, Muslim, and prosperous at the same time.

Premiering five years after *Noor, Magnificent Century* displays Turkey's growing economic power, cultural sophistication, and wealth. It is the most expensive TV program in Turkish history. Producers spend roughly $500,000 per episode, twice the amount that is spent on other serials. The program's launch party was held in Cannes, France. Its set is a lavish fifteen-room re-creation of Istanbul's Topkapi Palace, with real marble floors, handcrafted woodwork, and mock Ottoman and European throne rooms. Actors wear exquisite silk and velvet gowns crafted by a leading Turkish costume designer. Two siblings, known as the Coen brothers of Turkey, Durul and Yagmur Taylan, direct it.

"It's never been done before," Durul Taylan told me during a tour of the studio. "Not in this way."

In interviews, the directors and actors of *Magnificent Century* insisted the show was apolitical. "There is no political message or any other cultural message," said Ergenc, the actor who plays Suleiman. "This is a TV series. It is a soap opera."

Intentionally or not, the makers of Turkey's soap operas are creating new roles, new heroes, and new cultural norms in a rapidly changing region. I applaud them.

Turkey's political and economic influence in the region is on the rise as well. Erdogan was an early and vocal supporter of the Arab Spring uprisings. And after the toppling of dictators in Tunisia, Egypt, and Libya, he took a September 2011 victory tour of the region.

First, Erdogan and 260 Turkish businessmen made a historic

visit to post-Mubarak Egypt. In a single day, the businessmen announced $853 million in new contracts with Egyptian companies. One of them, Davut Dogan, promised to build a new $10 million furniture manufacturing center.

"The factory will employ two hundred people," Dogan boasted in an interview several weeks later in Istanbul.

From the rapturous welcome Erdogan received to the economic power the Turkish businessmen displayed, the trip demonstrated Turkey's rise as a regional power. After visiting Cairo, Erdogan continued to Tunis and Tripoli. In all three newly liberated post–Arab Spring capitals, Erdogan did something that no American can do. The Turkish leader told captivated audiences that Islam and democracy could coexist. The devout Muslim head of a conservative, Islamist political party said Muslims could be pious and democratic.

"Islam and democracy are not contradictory," Erdogan declared in Tunis. "A Muslim can run a state very successfully."

One of the most popular leaders in the Middle East, Erdogan has vastly more credibility in the region than the United States does. Rightly or wrongly, he has turned himself into a folk hero by lambasting Israel in recent years. And his success at creating jobs is widely admired in countries desperate for economic growth.

Erdogan somehow thwarted two political dynamics that have haunted the region: ineffectual democracy and repressive military rule. To the amazement of many, he broke the grip of Turkey's military, which overthrew three civilian governments between 1960 and 1980. And his party became such a dominant force in Turkey's fractious political system that it ended a long series of weak coalition governments.

In 2011 elections, Erdogan's party won a third term with 49 percent of the vote, a historically high vote total in Turkey's multiparty political system. In 2012, a parliamentary committee began drafting a new constitution to replace the one that had been drafted after a 1980 military coup.

Mustafa Akyol, a Turkish newspaper columnist and frequent Erdogan defender, said the prime minister's Justice and Development Party, known by its Turkish initials, AKP, is a model for Islamist parties in post–Arab Spring countries. Akyol argued in his 2011 book, *Islam Without Extremes: A Muslim Case for Liberty*, that there can be liberalism within Islam and challenges the authoritarian interpretations of Iran, Saudi Arabia, and militant groups.

"We can speak of an AKP model for other Islamic parties—and that's a good model," Akyol said in an interview. "If more and more Islamists are inspired by the AKP model than by the totalitarian example of Iran, that will be good for the region."

Davut Dogan, the Turkish furniture magnate who traveled to Egypt with Erdogan, embodies the AKP's economic transformation of Turkey. The fifty-one-year-old's family furniture company is one of the so-called Anatolian tigers—burgeoning firms that have risen from Turkey's conservative heartland.

More religious, driven, and ruthless than the genteel Istanbul elite, Anatolian businessmen have helped fuel Turkey's economic surge. Dogan's company, Dogtas, has opened 108 stylish, IKEA-like stores across the country catering to upwardly mobile, smartphone-wielding middle-class Turks.

Dogtas has experienced extraordinary growth in the last five years, with sales revenues and employees doubling to $200 million and 1,000, respectively. The firm, launched thirty-nine years ago as a family business, now exports to sixty-five countries and plans to continue its aggressive expansion in the Middle East, where it already has twelve shops in Iran, seven in Libya, five in Syria, and two in Iraq.

"We want to be as big in Egypt," said Dogan, "as we are in these other countries."

Bulent Celebi represents another type of growth in Turkey: high tech. Celebi, like Monis Rahman, the founder of Pakistan's first dating Web site, was profiled by American journalist Elmira Bayrasli in her magazine story on entrepreneurs in emerging market countries. Like Rahman, Celebi represents the intersection of technology, entrepreneurship, and globalization.

Istanbul is one of the world's most beautiful cities. It is also one of its most electronically impenetrable, Bayrasli wrote. The city's oldest houses are made of dense concrete that blocks the signals emitted by wireless routers designed for American drywall.

Sensing an opportunity, Celebi founded AirTies in 2004, an Istanbul technology start-up that develops and markets wireless electronic devices for specialized environments. After growing up in Istanbul, Celebi had moved to the United States and founded the chip company Ubicom in San Francisco, but memories of Istanbul and a business idea brought him home.

Celebi set out to create WiFi for the rest of the world. A WiFi box, just like a radio, streams a standard WiFi signal worldwide. But a standard American WiFi doesn't work everywhere, according to Bayrasli, a fact that wireless giants Linksys, D-Link, and Netgear had not yet realized. Focused on the American market, none of these companies were updating their devices for global markets. In San Francisco, Celebi encouraged these companies to adapt their devices for emerging markets, which he believed would boom. When the companies ignored his advice, he set out to do it himself.

Using contacts he had developed in San Francisco, Celebi raised $300,000 in seed capital from Silicon Valley investors and persuaded a handful of American-trained Turkish engineers to join him,

Bayrasli wrote. First, Celebi concentrated on Istanbul, where the concrete floors and walls weakened a continuous wireless signal.

To solve the problem, he developed a mesh technology that sent out repeated pulses like a beating heart. Electronic devices were able to pick up the pulses without interruption, giving the user a better signal. That became Celebi's trademark, according to Bayrasli.

At the same time, he focused on service and customization, an area where Linksys and others also lagged. Targeting Turkey, the Balkans, and the Middle East, a combined market of 465 million, he created routers with manuals and twenty-four-hour customer support in Turkish, Arabic, Bulgarian, Greek, Kazakh, and Romanian, Bayrasli wrote. Then he added Russian, which, together with Ukrainian, added another 187 million potential customers.

In Turkey, Celebi's business quickly expanded beyond Istanbul to Anatolia, where telephones had become widespread only in the mid-1980s and cable did not reach televisions until the 1990s. For decades, Turkey had been considered a creative, technological, and economic laggard, according to Bayrasli. Through centuries of Ottoman rule, Turks had relegated trade, commerce, and business to Armenians, Greeks, and Jews.

In modern Turkey, other problems emerged. Nepotism, red tape, weak rule of law, and a lack of investors and talent stifled Turkish markets, as they do in much of the developing world, Bayrasli wrote. Exhaustive bookkeeping to comply with Turkish tax laws and countless slips of paper that required business owners' personal authorization did as well. Last, under Turkish law, AirTies was Celebi's personal responsibility, according to Bayrasli. There was no limited liability or protection. If the company failed, he and his family lost everything.

Starting in the 1990s, in an effort to finally secure a spot in the European Union, Turkey's rulers slashed the country's bureaucracy and made it easier for Turks to register businesses, acquire licenses, build trade, and move capital freely in and out of the country. Turkish cotton traders struck deals with Levi's and Tommy Hilfiger. Anatolian furniture manufacturers like Dogtas signed deals with European conglomerates. Investment poured in, and a middle class was born. In a virtuous circle, Turkey's emerging middle class allowed Celebi to push entrepreneurship further.

Before becoming a senior adviser to Richard Holbrooke, Vali Nasr described the process in a 2009 book, *Forces of Fortune: The Rise of the New Muslim Middle Class and What It Will Mean for Our World*.

"Economic power shifted to small- and medium-sized businesses," Nasr wrote, "and the Anatolian heartland overshadowed Istanbul as an engine of growth."

Today AirTies dominates the wireless router market in the region, boasting 50 percent of the wireless market share in Turkey alone, Bayrasli wrote. It generates millions in revenues and is planning on an initial public offering in the next few years.

Today Turkey is the world's seventeenth-largest economy— bigger than all but six of the twenty-seven actual EU nations that have kept Turkey waiting for accession for forty-nine years. To many Turks, EU membership is no longer important. They see their future in the global market.

Critics of Erdogan warn that Turkey's phenomenal growth could stall. The AKP and the Anatolian tigers are creating a corrupt and insular political and economic elite that will eventually slow growth, they say. Behind closed doors, the government is steering lucrative projects to companies with links to senior party officials and creating an enormous AKP patronage mill.

Soli Ozel, a professor of international relations at Kadir Has

University in Istanbul, suspects that Erdogan may move toward "electoral authoritarianism." Elections will be held in Turkey, but the outcome will never be in doubt. Ozel warned that continued political and economic paralysis in the West could make the high growth and one-party rule of China increasingly appealing around the world.

"Unless the West gets out of its current economic malaise, it will be like the 1930s," Ozel predicted. "Democracy will lose its allure. Authoritarianism is going to have a feast."

Erdogan has suggested that Turkey's new constitution adopt a presidential system of government. If it does, the Turkish leader, who has said he will not serve again as prime minister after his third term ends in 2015, could rule Turkey as an all-powerful, Putin-like president.

There is another path for Erdogan. The drafting of a new constitution is an opportunity for him to strengthen Turkey, not his own rule. Increasing rights for minorities could ease the Kurdish insurgency, which has claimed forty thousand lives since the 1980s. Constitutional checks and balances that disperse power—instead of concentrating it—could restore faith in Erdogan's commitment to democracy. And the country's burgeoning middle class could be a source of stability for Turkey and the region for years.

Two contradictory Turkeys are emerging. One is a prosperous, modern nation that is a model for the region. The other is a popular but paranoid elected government that jails its perceived enemies by the hundreds.

As the civil war in Syria intensified, tensions rose inside Turkey. In November 2012, the number of Syrian refugees accepted by Turkey topped 120,000. Businessmen complained of lost trade and growing refugee camps. And after Kurdish separatists launched a series of attacks, Erdogan jailed several thousand more people, including writers, academics, elected mayors, and students, on charges of association with Kurdish separatists.

Turkish observers warned that the Kurdish insurgency was the biggest danger to the country's stability. If Erdogan failed to make a bold offer to begin a dialogue, the conflict could destabilize Turkey.

The United States should pressure Erdogan to abide by democratic norms and follow Europe's example. After the collapse of the Soviet Union in 1989, Europe followed a clear set of policies in Turkey for fifteen years. Offering incentives for the creation of free markets, modern judicial systems, and democratic institutions allowed Turkey to reform on its own terms.

The process was slow and involved repeated setbacks. As recently as 2002, Turkey was mired in recession and debt. In 2013, its economic growth is likely to slow. But Turkey represents the ability of Western technology, consumerism, entrepreneurship, and investment to transform a country. And, unlike Iraq and Afghanistan, it is a potentially powerful example of a new interpretation of Islam fashioned by Muslims, not outsiders.

CHAPTER 6

The Silicon Valley of the Arab World?

In June 2009, President Obama called for "a new beginning" between the United States and the Muslim world in a historic speech at Cairo University. No one present—including Obama—had any sense of the sweeping changes about to be unleashed across the region.

In his speech, Obama called for mutual respect, the spread of democracy, and peace between Israelis and Palestinians. As millions of Arabs watched, he also promised revitalized economic aid.

"On economic development, we will create a new corps of business volunteers to partner with counterparts in Muslim-majority countries," Obama said. "And I will host a Summit on Entrepreneurship this year to identify how we can deepen ties between business leaders, foundations, and social entrepreneurs in the United States and Muslim communities around the world."

In April 2010, the administration held the promised summit in Washington and launched a series of programs to send American businessmen, investors, and scientists to the Middle East. Eight months later, a twenty-six-year-old Tunisian street vendor named Mohamed Bouazizi doused himself in gasoline on December 10, set himself on fire, and sparked the Arab Spring.

The protests, though, were not as spontaneous as they seemed. For months, unemployment and food prices had been rising in Tunisia as the global economy slowed. And the November 2010 release by WikiLeaks of secret American diplomatic cables detailing staggering corruption by Tunisian President Zine el-Abidine Ben Ali stoked popular anger as well. The cables also gave protesters the sense that American support for Ben Ali was waning.

Twenty-eight days after the largely peaceful protests began, Ben Ali fled the country. Obama, who felt that he had been too passive during the June 2009 uprising in Iran, made no effort to help Ben Ali. The president's move was both courageous and practical. Tunisia, a small country that was not strategically important to the United States, was a low-risk place to support a revolution. Few American officials thought the uprisings would spread.

Secretary of State Hillary Clinton and European diplomats praised the revolution but offered limited financial support to the country's new government. European Union countries pledged $300 million in direct assistance. The Obama administration, which saw Tunisia as Europe's responsibility, offered roughly the same amount.

Ten months after Ben Ali's ouster, the American embassy announced that a delegation of American high-tech entrepreneurs and angel investors would be visiting Tunisia. American officials, it seemed, were delivering on Obama's promise in Cairo to bring U.S. entrepreneurs to the region. The group would hold a workshop on launching start-ups, listen to attendees' business proposals, and then choose one Tunisian for training and mentoring in the United States.

The response was overwhelming. Dozens of Tunisian entrepreneurs, programmers, and engineers applied to attend the session. Each applicant submitted a written proposal for a new start-up. The organizers then invited the authors of the fifty best proposals to attend.

From beginning to end, the workshop overflowed with energy. Young Tunisians clamored to speak with the American entrepreneurs and investors. When a young woman's proposal for a biotech start-up was finally chosen as the winner, other attendees were disappointed. Privately, members of the American delegation were disappointed as well.

In truth, the post-Cairo initiative that brought them to Tunisia operated on a shoestring. The program—Partners for a New Beginning—was so poorly funded that members of the delegation had to pay their own airfare and hotel bills. The U.S. government did not propose, fund, or carry out the training of the winning entrepreneur. Members of the delegation did. And the prize? Three months in the TechTown incubator in Detroit, Michigan, courtesy of Tech-Town, Wayne State University, and the American Arab Chamber of Commerce in Detroit.

One member of the delegation, Sami Ben Romdhane, a Tunisian American eBay executive, was shocked by the lack of funding. A founder of two Silicon Valley start-ups and former Apple and Oracle employee, Ben Romdhane was impressed by the talent pool in Tunisia.

"There is a lot of potential," Ben Romdhane said in a telephone interview after his visit. "I don't see any difference between students who are graduating there and students who are graduating here and in Europe."

The administration's tepid effort showed how the United States was missing an opportunity in Tunisia to create a post–Arab Spring success story. More broadly, it was evidence that the administration was taking the wrong lessons from Afghanistan, Iraq, and Pakistan and squandering the opportunity that the Arab Spring created.

In interviews, Tunisians embraced Obama's message in Cairo. Asked what the United States could do to help Tunisia, they called for increased American business investment, tourism, and educational exchange programs, not traditional foreign aid.

Without prompting, they disparaged hard-line Salafists who had emerged since the toppling of Ben Ali in January 2011. Declaring themselves a model for the rest of the Middle East, Tunisians said they yearned for prosperity, modernity, and a place in the global economy.

Public opinion polls showed a mixed view of the United States. A 2012 survey found that 90 percent of Tunisians wanted democracy in their country but believed that the United States had not supported their revolution. A year after Obama's Cairo speech, only 40 percent of Tunisians had a positive view of the U.S. president. In Washington, Obama himself was disappointed by how few of his promises in Cairo had been turned into functioning programs. The government's weak civilian institutions had again failed at implementation.

"Obama later conceded that the speech was longer on promises than on deliverables," journalist David E. Sanger wrote in his 2012 book, *Confront and Conceal*. "A year later, when he asked for an assessment of how well the administration had implemented the ideas he announced in Cairo, he was, in the words of one aide, "deeply disappointed in how little got done."

In Tunisia, meanwhile, the country's postrevolution economy collapsed. In 2011, the growth rate dropped from 3 percent to -1.8 percent, inflation nearly doubled to 5 percent, foreign investment declined by 30 percent, and the country's tourism industry disappered. In 2012, the economy improved somewhat, growing at 2.7 percent, but Tunisia's growth remained half the 5 percent growth it enjoyed between 1997 and 2007.

The Islamist political party that won the country's first post–Ben Ali elections—Ennahda, or the "Renaissance Party"—struggled to effectively run the government after decades in exile. The party's charismatic leader was Rached Ghannouchi, a seventy-year-old Sorbonne-educated Islamist intellectual who had spent fourteen years in Tunisian prisons and twenty-two years in exile in London.

In an interview, Ghannouchi described his Ennahda party as a moderate Islamist movement modeled after Turkish Prime Minister Erdogan's AKP party. He said he fervently supported democracy, a stand that put him at odds with radical Salafists who consider democracy an affront to God's authority. Echoing Turkish moderates, he said democracy and Islam were not only compatible, they follow the same traditions.

"The real spokesman of Islam is public opinion, which is the high authority, the highest authority," he said. "Legislation, represented by the assembly, the national assembly."

Ghannouchi said the prophet Muhammad's use of *shuras*—or councils—to make nonreligious decisions showed that democracy had existed in Islam since its birth. Government affairs should be decided by democratic vote, he said, not fatwas from religious autocrats. And he embraced free-market capitalism, full rights for women and minorities, and international human rights treaties.

Secular Tunisians, though, say that Ghannouchi's party has not followed those ideals since gaining power. The country's new draft constitution has a blasphemy law in it that makes insulting any of the three Abrahamic faiths a crime. To secular Tunisians, this is a clear limit on free speech.

In February 2012, the party stood by when a Tunisian judge jailed a newspaper editor for eight days after he published a photograph of a soccer player and his nude girlfriend on the cover of a local tabloid. And in April 2012, two young men were sentenced to seven years in jail for posting cartoons of a nude prophet Muhammad on Facebook.

Secular Tunisians said they no longer trust Ennahda. Ahmed Ounaies, a Tunisian politician who briefly served as foreign minister in the country's postrevolutionary unity government, was typical. In an interview, he said he no longer believed Ghannouchi. He believed that purportedly moderate Muslim leaders were, in fact, aligned with hard-line Islamists.

"We believe that Mr. Ghannouchi is a Salafist," Ounaies said. "He is a real supporter of those groups."

Amid the political and economic turmoil, hard-line Tunisian Salafists have became increasingly emboldened. In 2011, they attacked a television station in Tunis after it aired the animated film *Persepolis,* which featured what they considered a blasphemous portrayal of God. They attacked liquor stores and art galleries. They held protests that paralyzed the country's leading university for a month. And in the capital they climbed a historic bell tower and waved jihadist flags from its spire—an image that unnerved Tunisian moderates and foreign investors.

Clashes and demonstrations have continued in 2012. In May, one of the country's new Salafist groups, Ansar al-Shariah, held a rally in the religious city of Kairouan. At the event, Salafists dressed in the style of Afghan Taliban staged martial arts demonstrations and horsemen brandished swords.

In June, they attacked an art exhibit in Tunis, setting off clashes across the country and a three-day curfew. And after the amateur video insulting the prophet Muhammad emerged in September 2012, several thousand Salafists attacked the American embassy in Tunis and burned down the adjacent American school. The following day, the State Department announced that the families of all American diplomats and other nonessential personnel would be evacuated from the country.

The news devastated secular Tunisians. They were furious at Tunisia's new government for failing to deploy enough police to protect the embassy. And they were surprised that the United States reacted so drastically to a protest by a small faction of Tunisians.

Sami Ben Romdhane, the Tunisian American eBay executive, said Tunisians who prided themselves on being one of the most liberal societies in the Middle East felt abandoned.

"Now it's official," Ben Romdhane told me. "We are being treated as a terrorist country and a place where Americans are not safe. That hurt a lot of people in the country."

Tunisian moderates argued that the United States was missing an opportunity in Tunisia. America's strongest weapons against militancy were engagement, investment, and technology, they said. Young Tunisians yearned to work in the new, high-tech offices that Hewlett-Packard, Fidelity, Microsoft, and Cisco opened in Tunisia in recent years. They dreamed of turning their country into a regional hub for cloud, big-data, and open-government computing.

Leila Charfi, the head of the Microsoft Innovation Center in Tunis, helped organize the visit by the American high-tech delegation. She said Facebook and Twitter had facilitated the street protests that toppled Ben Ali, and that Tunisians now embraced technology. "People are hungry to use new technology and develop a new country with IT," she said.

But after the attack on the American embassy, investors from Silicon Valley and Europe saw Tunisia as unstable and anti-American, according to Ben Romdhane.

"They're asking, 'What happened? How come this country changed in eighteen months and became like Libya?'" Ben Romdhane said. "I keep saying, 'This is not representative. This is a fraction of a percent of people.'"

The shift in perception is tragic. Prior to the embassy attack, American diplomats declared that Tunisia had the brightest long-term prospects of any Arab Spring country. It has an ethnically homogeneous population of only 10 million, a long history of moderation, and centuries of trade with Europe that have created a strong business class and millions of bilingual Arabic and French speakers.

Most important, the country's lack of oil forced it to develop a multifaceted economy after it achieved independence from France in 1956. Its universities graduate six thousand engineers a year, and Tunisian entrepreneurs managed to develop niche markets in Europe. Inspired by Jean Touitou, the Tunisian-born designer and founder of the French clothing line A.P.C., Tunisian factories cornered the market on rush orders from Europe for high-quality clothes. Tunisian auto-parts factories produced high-quality components for Mercedes-Benz and other elite car manufacturers. And the country's farms provided Europe with everything from fresh vegetables to olive oil.

Like that of Turkey, Tunisia's economy eventually became closely tied to that of Europe. France, the former colonial power, was Tunisia's largest foreign investor. As a result, when the European sovereign debt crisis exploded in 2010, Tunisia was one of the victims. As European orders and investment dropped, unemployment and food prices rose in Tunisia. Europe offered little aid to Tunisia as well. The tepid postrevolutionary economy exacerbated a festering economic divide between Tunisia's wealthy coast and impoverished interior. When I visited Tunisia fourteen months after the revolution, in March 2012, I found pockets of simmering anger and a deep sense of unmet expectations. Tunisians who had expected a postrevolutionary gold rush held protests and wildcat strikes on a daily basis.

In the southern town of Gafsa, unemployed people blocked roads to the town's phosphate mine, the fifth largest in the world, and demanded jobs. Production had dropped by 40 percent. After wildcat strikes by local workers, a Japanese company shut down its local factory. A German company threatened to do the same.

Even in Sidi Bouzid, the farming town where Tunisia's uprising began, the luster of the revolution had faded. The manager of a call center that a French investor had opened to help support the revolution complained of constant confrontations with workers. Whenever she tried to fire someone, their parents came to the office and berated her. Strikes occurred constantly at other businesses, she said, sowing chaos.

On a dusty street, eighty-five-year-old Ahmad Kadachi said he was also disillusioned. The dean of the town's street vendors, Kadachi had been astonished when Bouazizi, the local vendor, had set himself on fire and sparked the Arab Spring.

As Kadachi sold tea from his ramshackle wooden cart, he called Bouazizi a hothead, but thanked him for the freedom he had brought. Now, Kadachi said, he was frustrated with postrevolutionary Tunisia. He said Tunisians, Egyptians, and Libyans enjoyed being able to choose their leaders and express their opinions, but a primary goal of their revolutions eluded them: prosperity.

"Everybody is talking and talking," Kadachi told me. "No one is doing anything."

In Tunis, the country's cosmopolitan capital, the verdict on the revolution was more positive. Khalil Zahouani, a thirty-four-year-old

Tunisian entrepreneur, said the ouster of Ben Ali had perfectly positioned Tunisia to follow India's example and become an outsourcing hub for the region. With millions of well-educated French speakers, Tunisia could become the French-speaking world's back office, Zahouani said. In Tunisia, software companies, call centers, and engineering firms could perform tasks at a fraction of the cost of Europe.

Zahouani's own experience was an example. After graduating from a Swiss university and working in Geneva for several years, he returned to Tunisia to start his own business. Like Monis Rahman, the American-educated Pakistani entrepreneur who returned home to start Pakistan's first online dating site, Zahouani believed that his chances of creating a fast-growing technology company were higher in Tunisia than in Europe. When I met him in Tunis, Zahouani ran a seventy-person start-up that provided computing services to European and Arab phone conglomerates.

His firm, Dot IT, is based in Les Berges du Lac, one of Tunis's priciest neighborhoods. It felt global. Young, cigarette-smoking Tunisian couples clad in stylish French clothes filled a nearby bistro. A sushi restaurant was a few blocks away.

As Zahouani spoke excitedly of his business plan, several dozen young men and women clad in Western clothes worked intently at their computers. Some women wore headscarves. Some did not.

"We can have centers for excellence for IBM, Apple, and Google for the region," Zahouani predicted. "It could be an outsourcing hub."

A few miles away, Hewlett-Packard, the Palo Alto, California–based computing giant, and SunGard, a Wayne, Pennsylvania–based software company, share a sparkling new office building. With subsidies from the Ben Ali government, the two companies built an ultramodern office complex several years ago. On the building's ground floor was a gym with yoga classes, a gleaming new cafeteria, and an employee lounge with a large-screen television. Workers were dressed casually in jeans and button-down shirts. Young Tunisians from across the country competed fiercely to work at the two firms. Both were seen as doorways to the global economy.

In SunGard's lobby, clocks displayed the current time in the company's Tunis, New York, and Pune, India, offices. Worldwide, SunGard had seventeen thousand employees in seventy countries. Last year, it earned roughly $4.5 billion providing software and processing services for financial companies, governments, and educational institutions.

In Tunis, its five hundred employees performed back-office work for French- and English-speaking customers in Europe, Asia, and North America. It was also a beachhead for the company in the 200-million-strong Middle Eastern market.

Adel Torjmen, SunGard's managing director in Tunisia, said private investment from American companies was much more valuable than American government development aid.

"What the U.S. can bring is very clear," he said. "The savior of Tunisia cannot be the government of the United States. It is the private sector."

Torjmen, a Tunisian engineer educated in France, said the problem was not that Tunisia had a negative image in the United States. It was that it had no image at all in the United States. American companies do not think of the Middle East, he said, when they consider outsourcing. If IBM moved only 15 percent of its 150,000 employees in India to Tunisia, he said, it would make a vast difference in the country's economy.

"Tunisia can be yet another Dubai but addressing Europe and Africa," he said. "Our cost structure is better than Morocco and we are close to India. Try to give us a kind of privilege, a kind of chance."

Radhi Meddeb, a French- and Italian-educated Tunisian engineer who heads the Action and Solidarity Development Association, a leading Tunisian nonprofit development group, said American business expertise was needed as well. Meddeb said Tunisia needed help restructuring its banking sector, creating a microfinance system, forming public-private partnerships to build infrastructure, and creating a private equity fund.

He called for a $25 billion American investment over the next seven to ten years in modernizing Tunisia's infrastructure. Someday, he hoped, Tunisia and the United States could sign a free-trade agreement.

Regarding Europe, Meddeb said Tunisia should voluntarily enact the reforms mandated in the EU accession process but not expect admission, given Europe's financial crisis. The United States and Europe had promised $20 billion in aid to Tunisia and Egypt at the 2011 G8 summit in Deauville, he said, but little of that money had arrived.

Meddeb and other Tunisians complained as the economy sputtered that the Ennahda-led government was spending enormous amounts of time debating the status of religion in the country's new constitution. Unlike Erdogan, who managed the Turkish economy deftly, Ennahda seems overwhelmed. Secular Tunisians said Ennahda needed to crack down on the Salafists immediately.

Ghannouchi, Ennahda's leader, played down the country's divisions and called for patience.

"I am not pessimistic," he said in the interview. "There is a chance to reach a compromise."

In the United States, many Americans simply do not trust the Islamists. They believe that after gaining power, Ennahda and other Islamist parties will insert Islam into school curriculums, roll back women's rights, and reduce individual freedoms. Some Israelis fear that Ennahda will follow the route of Hamas, the Islamist movement that won elections in Gaza and Islamized local institutions after years of relatively secular Fatah rule.

The United States needs to engage more with Tunisia's Islamists, not less. So far, the Obama administration has provided $300 million in aid to Tunisia—and $100 million of it is for Tunisian government budget support since the January 2011 revolution. The American effort should be larger and more innovative.

Compared with Iraq and Afghanistan, the American civilian aid effort in Tunisia is minuscule. State Department officials are overreacting to their expensive failures in Afghanistan, Iraq, and Pakistan and shifting to a minimalist extreme.

In conversations, American diplomats in Tunis focused on limiting their aid efforts and engaging in only traditional diplomacy. Many of them had served in Iraq or Afghanistan and apparently saw the aid programs there as wasteful aberrations that departed from the State Department's true diplomatic mission.

They are wrong. The State Department and other civilian agencies must learn how to devise, properly fund, and implement programs like the one that brought Ben Romdhane and the other Arab American entrepreneurs to Tunis. Facilitating investment, entrepreneurship, and educational exchanges on a vast scale should be a core element of the State Department's mission. The Tunisian businessmen I spoke with were correct. American investment, consumerism, and technology are our most powerful tools against militancy. The United States should be confident of those weapons and not fear Ennahda and other moderate Islamist parties.

In interviews, Tunisian Islamists said they did not want American meddling in their political affairs, but they were eager to be part of the world economy. Becoming Hamas-like international pariahs seemed to hold little appeal for them. They too know that a by-product of a globalized economy is that isolation now carries a staggering economic cost.

Asked what U.S. policies would most help Muslim moderates, Ennahda founder Ghannouchi echoed secular Tunisians. He called for the U.S. government to "encourage investment," "encourage tourism," and sharply expand training and educational exchange programs. Asked what U.S. policies were most destructive, he said that unilateral U.S. military interventions undermine Muslim moderates.

A week after I visited Tunisia, three hundred people packed a Carnegie Endowment conference in Washington where Islamists from Tunisia, Egypt, Libya, Morocco, and Jordan tried to explain their views and goals. Americans asked Islamists if their commitment to democracy was real. Islamists asked the same question back. Some exchanges were tense, but an awkward dialogue began.

CHAPTER 7

Murder in Benghazi

In September 2011, Mark Ward, a fifty-seven-year-old senior USAID official, arrived in Tripoli after spending much of the last decade in Afghanistan and Pakistan. Ward, a San Francisco native, father of two sons, and former lawyer had seen the mistakes of the American effort in Afghanistan and Pakistan firsthand. In Libya, he was determined to get the American aid effort right.

From 2002 to 2003, Ward had served as USAID mission director in Pakistan. In 2005, he returned to Pakistan to coordinate US-AID's response to a devastating earthquake in the country's north. From 2006 to 2008, Ward lived in Washington and served as the agency's head of procurement, overseeing its army of contractors in Afghanistan and Iraq. From 2008 to 2010, he was seconded to the UN and moved to Kabul while serving as the organization's senior adviser for development.

In 2009, Ward narrowly survived a Taliban attack on the UN guesthouse where he lived in Kabul. Five UN staff and three Afghans were killed. Ward and twenty-five other survivors owed their lives to a young American who worked as Ward's UN security guard. Louis Maxwell, a twenty-seven-year-old father of two and former navy sailor from Florida, grabbed his weapon as soon as the attack began. Running to the roof, Maxwell held off three suicide bombers who were trying to enter the compound. After Ward and two dozen others fled, Maxwell was shot dead.

"He was a wonderful guy," Ward recalled. "He really was a hero. I told my boys there are not many of us who get to meet a real hero and I did."

Ward arrived in Tripoli in September 2011 and immediately warmed to Libya and Libyans. He spent the next thirteen months advising UN, American, and European officials on how to better coordinate foreign aid projects. In Afghanistan, a free-for-all had ensued. With little to no input from Afghan officials, foreign countries built hundreds of projects that impressed their bosses back home but didn't necessarily aid Afghans. With no coordinated strategy, waste was endemic.

Two things in Libya immediately struck Ward as completely different from Afghanistan. The country was overflowing with oil wealth. As a result, Libyan officials did not hesitate to tell foreign officials what was on their minds.

"The transitional government officials that I worked with were very capable of saying no," Ward recalled, "to what they perceived as a bad idea."

Libya has an estimated 46 billion barrels of oil, one of the largest reserves in the world. Its population is small but well educated, with a 89 percent literacy rate among its 6.7 million people. During and after the uprising against Qaddafi, the United States and other countries gave the country's interim government control of $100 billion in Libyan government and Qaddafi family assets seized abroad.

The differences between Libya and Afghanistan leapt out at Ward. In Kabul, he had watched in frustration as Afghan officials said yes to expensive foreign aid projects that their government would be unable to maintain in the future. In Tripoli, Libyan officials promised to reimburse the U.S. government for any training they received.

"They said we need U.S. expertise, not your money," Ward recalled.

And when a foreigner pushed too far, the Libyans made their feelings clear.

"I used to tell people, 'From my own personal experience, we've got to just chill here,'" Ward told me. "The way we are going to build trust with the Libyans is listening to them."

Some foreign diplomats ignored his advice. Others completely agreed. One senior diplomat who shared Ward's go-slow approach was the new U.S. ambassador to Libya, J. Christopher Stevens.

Stevens, like Ward, was a Northern California native and former lawyer who became a diplomat. While Ward focused on South Asia, Stevens spent twenty years working across the Middle East. In 2011, Stevens had lived with rebels in Benghazi and made sure that U.S. aid reached the Libyan opposition. Ward and Stevens both spent hours talking to Libyans and trying to understand the country.

"He represented what you hoped would be the model of a new American diplomat," Ward said. "He was much happier rolling his sleeves up and going to work and talking to Libyans."

The Libyans were deeply suspicious of the United States and Europe. After decades of being an international pariah, Qaddafi was embraced by President George W. Bush and British Prime Minister Tony Blair in 2004 after halting Libya's nuclear weapons program and handing over its chemical weapons. In 2006, the United States established full diplomatic relations with the Libyan government, turning a blind eye to nearly forty years of brutal Qaddafi family rule.

Behind the scenes, Blair had helped negotiate oil exploration deals worth at least $500 million for the British conglomerate Royal Dutch Shell. U.S. oil companies descended on Libya as well, along with other Americans in search of profit. Monitor, a Boston-based consulting group run by Harvard Business School professors, received $3 million from the Qaddafi regime from 2006 to 2008 to help rehabilitate Qaddafi's image in the United States.

Monitor paid travel expenses, consulting fees, and honorariums to conservative American scholars such as Francis Fukuyama and Richard Perle, as well as liberals like Benjamin Barber, Joseph Nye, and Robert Putnam. At Monitor's expense the prominent Americans visited Qaddafi and wrote stories about him. The firm also helped ghostwrite the PhD thesis of one of Qaddafi's son's, Saif, at the London School of Economics.

Qaddafi's repression, meanwhile, continued. For forty-two years, Qaddafi ruled by pitting Libyans against one another. An estimated 10 to 20 percent of the population served in various overlapping surveillance directorates that monitored Libyans in government agencies, factories, and schools. The police state extended beyond Libya. During the 1980s, a network of diplomats and recruits killed twenty-five opponents of Qaddafi in foreign countries.

Over the years, Qaddafi's behavior grew more bizarre. In 2009, he gave a ninety-minute speech to the United Nations General Assembly in New York. At different points in the rambling address, he called for the reinvestigation of the killings of John F. Kennedy and Martin Luther King Jr., the creation of a joint Israeli-Palestinian state called "Isratine," and hailed Barack Obama, whom he called a "son of Africa."

"Obama is a glimpse in the darkness after four or eight years," he said. "We are content and happy if Obama can stay forever as president of the United States."

After Qaddafi's death in 2011, President Obama issued clear orders that the United States should not lead the postwar stabilization effort in Libya. In Tripoli, European diplomats coordinated the international effort while U.S. diplomats took a secondary role. It was an example of Obama's belief in focusing American resources on direct threats to the United States and handing over responsibility to allies when possible.

"What I saw was a United States that was in listening mode, that was very much waiting for the Libyans to say, 'This is where we need help,'" Ward recalled. "And resisting what maybe is our more traditional approach, which is supply side assistance, 'This is what you need, and we have it, so can we provide it?'"

One final dynamic that was different from Afghanistan was that of security contractors. After seeing reports of their aggressive behavior, Libyan officials blocked the United States from using firms like Blackwater to protect its diplomats. The CIA and State Department hired a dozen private contractors to roam the country and buy looted anti-aircraft missiles that could fall into the hands of militants. But security contractors were barred.

While Tunisia was a victim of its success and relative stability, Libya was a victim of its past and lack of national institutions. Before and after Qaddafi's death, analysts predicted that the country's myriad tribes would descend into civil war. And there are growing fears that hard-line Islamists will dominate the country.

Like Tunisia, Libya had an Islamist underground that sent fighters to Afghanistan and, later, Iraq to fight Soviet and American forces. For decades, Libyan Islamists were the focus of brutal government crackdowns. In a bizarre turn of events, one leader of the uprising against Qaddafi spent five years in American detention in Guantánamo Bay, the *New York Times* reported. Abu

Sufian Ibrahim Ahmed Hamuda bin Qumu served as a tank driver in the Libyan army in the 1980s, according to the *Times*. In the 1990s, he journeyed to Afghanistan to join the anti-Soviet jihad. After the 9/11 attacks, Qumu was captured in Pakistan, flown to Guantánamo, and accused of being a member of the militant Libyan Islamist Fighting Group. All of the allegations against him were based on information provided by the Libyan government.

Qumu hailed from Darnah, a town famed for purportedly being the world's top recruiting ground for suicide bombers. An analysis of 600 suicide bombers in Iraq by the Combating Terrorism Center at West Point found that of 440 who had listed their hometowns in a recruiting roster, 52 were from Darnah, according to the *Times*. Riyadh, Saudi Arabia, a city with forty times the population, came in second, sending 51.

In 2007, American officials transferred Qumu to Libyan government custody. The following year, he was freed in a government amnesty.

Beyond the Islamist threat, Libya was plagued by tribal divisions. While Tunisia is relatively homogenous ethnically, Libya is a conglomeration of North African tribes that were cobbled together by colonial mapmakers. It lacks the strong national identities and revered national leaders that modern Turkey and Tunisia enjoyed in Mustafa Kemal Ataturk and Habib Bourguiba.

When the 2011 uprising against Qaddafi began, hundreds of militias formed along tribal lines. After his death, militias refused to disarm or hand over an estimated five thousand prisoners they had declared regime loyalists. Human rights groups gained access to some of the prisoners. Their stories were grim. Captives said the militias engaged in torture, held prisoners without evidence, and blocked detainees from seeing judges for up to a year.

The country's National Transitional Council—which Libyan exiles dominated—impressed Ward. The council's leaders moved cautiously, dealt with immediate crises, did not confront militias, and waited for an elected government to set policy. When firefights between rival militias broke out in parts of the country, the interim council dispatched envoys to negotiate truces.

The Transitional Council also embraced the emergence of Libyan women's, human rights, and press groups. They welcomed protests. During one of Ward's meetings with the deputy prime minister, gunfire erupted outside. The Libyan official smiled and said the shooting was a healthy sign.

"He sat back in his chair and he had this big smile on his face," Ward recalled. "He said, 'Isn't this great? This is what we fought for.'"

Four months after Ward left Libya, the country held its first free elections in four decades, in June 2012. More than three thousand candidates—including women—competed for two hundred seats in a new assembly. To the astonishment of many, a coalition of liberals led by National Transitional Council leader Mahmoud Jibril won thirty-nine of the eighty seats for political parties. Jibril's party even won in Darnah, the suicide bomber stronghold. The Muslim Brotherhood came in second, with seventeen.

How the new assembly will function remains unclear—120 seats are reserved for independent candidates with unknown loyalties.

When Ward completed his assignment and returned to Washington in February 2012, he believed the United States had struck the right balance in Libya. It was listening to the new government and waiting for it to make specific requests from the international community, something that rarely happened in Afghanistan, Iraq, and Pakistan. Ward credited Obama with setting the right tone. He said a UN colleague praised the United States for showing unusual restraint.

"The United States was handling this the right way," Ward recalled. "The United States can lead even when it's not leading."

At 9:15 P.M. on September 11, 2012, Ambassador Chris Stevens finished a meeting with the Turkish ambassador, walked him to the front gate of the American consulate in Benghazi, and bid him good night. Stevens briefly chatted with the compound's Libyan guards. Three were armed members of a local militia that had rebelled against the Qaddafi regime. Four were unarmed. Then Stevens returned to his residence.

Fifteen minutes later, the guards heard shouts of "God is great!" outside the compound. At first, they thought a funeral procession might have been passing by. Then one of them heard an American shouting, "Attack, attack," over the radio. Gunfire erupted and grenades began landing in the center of the compound.

In a carefully coordinated assault, several dozen members of Ansar al-Shariah, a well-known local militia consisting of hard-line Islamic militants, were attacking the compound. Armed with rocket-propelled grenades and truck-mounted artillery, they fired grenade after grenade into the compound.

"They thought that there would be more Americans inside, commandos or something like that," Mohamed Bishari, a twenty-year-old neighbor who watched the attack, told the *New York Times.* "So they immediately started attacking with their RPG rockets."

In truth, seven Americans were inside the compound and only four of them were armed. One of Mr. Stevens's bodyguards ran out of an office building holding a light weapon and sprinted to Stevens's residence under fire, according to Libyan guards. Two other armed Americans climbed on a rooftop and fought back against the attackers. So did the armed Libyan fighters.

Inside his residence, Stevens, a technician named Sean Smith, and Stevens's bodyguard locked themselves in a secure safe room. At some point, the attackers breached the compound, poured diesel around Stevens's residence, and set it ablaze.

What happened next is unclear. As thick smoke filled the safe room, the three Americans apparently tried to make a run for it. The bodyguard climbed out a window, but Stevens and Smith succumbed to the smoke and died of asphyxiation. In the chaos, guards found Smith's body but were unable to locate Stevens. Four hours later, two guards died in a carefully planned mortar attack in a CIA compound a mile away.

Stevens was the first American ambassador to be killed in an act of terrorism in twenty-three years. His death immediately became a heated issue in the 2012 presidential campaign. Republicans accused the Obama administration of failing to provide adequate security for American diplomats. They also accused the White House of trying to downplay the attack by initially calling it a spontaneous demonstration sparked by the amateur American-made anti-Muslim video. The Obama administration denied both charges.

Within twenty-four hours, the State Department pulled all of its diplomats out of Libya. The suffocating security that hindered the civilian effort in Afghanistan, Pakistan, and Iraq grew even more intense. What happened in Benghazi and how to respond to it consumed Washington.

* * *

Over the next several weeks, press reports and congressional investigations revealed that midlevel State Department officials had denied repeated requests for additional security in Benghazi as attacks rose in the summer of 2012. Barred from using contractors, the department's Diplomatic Security Service had such a small staff that it sent its personnel to Libya on three-month rotations.

At one point in the summer, the Benghazi compound had only one American guard. State Department officials said Benghazi was a symbol of a brittle, overstretched, and underfunded State Department.

When Ward learned of Stevens's death, he was dismayed but thought that Stevens's wishes would be clear.

"He would say to the American people, please don't turn your back on Libya," Ward told me. "They've been through forty terrible years, they've just held elections, and they've rejected extremism. This is absolutely not the time to let a couple of lunatics throw us off our resolve."

According to Ward, Stevens's message to Libyans would be to arrest the suspected perpetrators, provide them with defense lawyers, and give them a fair trial. "Do the right thing," Ward said. "If there is one thing [his] life should stand for, let it stand for the rule of law."

Fred Abrahams, a senior adviser with Human Rights Watch who frequently met with Stevens while working in Libya, agreed. He said Stevens wasn't naïve about Libya's problems but saw Qaddafi's overthrow as a historic opportunity to establish the rule of law Libyans longed for.

"Just as the U.S. should not be blamed for the offensive film of a few deluded whackos, Libya should not be blamed for the unjustified violence of a few ignorant extremists," Abrahams said. "Maybe this will spur the Libyan government to rein in the militias that have troubled Libya since Qaddafi's fall—Chris would have wanted that."

A week after Stevens's murder, Libyans did just that. An estimated thirty thousand Benghazi residents took to the streets of the city, protested Stevens's death, and called for the disbanding of militias. That night, protesters stormed the compound of Ansar al-Shariah and forced them to flee.

"We want police in the streets; we don't want the militia," Nisa Nejam, a twenty-one-year-old blogger and civil society activist who participated in the protest, said in a telephone interview. "We want all of them under the control of the government."

Three weeks before he died, Stevens reopened the American consulate in Tripoli and announced that visas would be issued to hundreds of Libyan businessmen, journalists, and students to visit the United States. He said that increasing trade, educational ties, and interaction between the two countries was vital.

"Relationships between governments are important, but relationships between people are the real foundation of mutual understanding," Stevens said. "So, my message to Libyans today is *ahlan wasahlan bikum*. You are welcome to visit America, and there's the door!"

We should open doors, not close them.

CHAPTER 8

Post-Mubarak

After returning to Washington in February 2012, Mark Ward was named special coordinator in the Office of Middle East Transition—a new State Department unit created to coordinate civilian aid to Egypt, Libya, and Tunisia.

On paper, the post put Ward in an ideal position to carry out Chris Stevens's work and apply the lessons he had learned in Afghanistan and Pakistan to post–Arab Spring countries. It also took him back to Egypt, the country where he started his career at USAID twenty-four years earlier.

The challenges, complexities, and pressures that Ward and his colleagues found in Cairo were staggering. While Obama had insisted that other European countries take the lead in Tunisia and Libya, both parties in Congress and Israel assumed that the United States would be the lead Western actor in post-Mubarak Egypt.

The people of Egypt, though, wanted nothing to do with the United States.

After forty years of living under American-backed dictators, 82 percent of Egyptians said in a September 2012 Gallup poll that they did not want to receive any type of assistance from the United

States. Egyptians, in fact, were more hostile toward the American aid than they were toward Egypt's peace treaty with Israel. In the Gallup poll, 42 percent of Egyptians said they opposed the peace treaty with Israel, roughly half the number who opposed accepting American aid.

How, then, could the United States forge a new relationship with a strategically important and unstable country clearly in need of multiple forms of assistance? First, it must avoid the mistakes of the past.

For the last thirty years, the United States' alliance with Israel made stabilizing Egypt—and maintaining the Camp David Accords— vital to the United States. Since the signing of the Accords in 1978, the United States had provided $40 billion in military aid and $28 billion in civilian aid to Egypt.

Current aid levels remain vast. In 2011, Washington gave the Egyptian army $1.5 billion in military aid and $250 million in civilian aid.

Unfortunately, the track record of American aid to Egypt has been disastrous. The military aid helped the Egyptian army run a vast for-profit business empire inside the country. Like the Pakistani army, it controlled large swaths of the Egyptian economy and ran scores of for-profit factories, farms, and other businesses. On the civilian side, USAID has carried out some successful development projects, but the overwhelming perception inside Egypt—and across the region—is that America was propping up a pro-American dictatorship to protect Israel, not helping the Egyptian people.

In a May 2012 Pew survey, 61 percent of Egyptians polled said they believed that American economic and military aid had a mostly negative impact on Egypt. Only 21 percent believed it had a mostly positive impact.

To be fair to USAID officials, much of the blame lies with the Mubarak government, which squandered billions in aid in the 1980s. In the 1990s, the Mubarak government finally carried out an IMF-backed economic reform plan that opened up the country's long state-driven economy and sparked growth rates of up to 5 percent.

It also produced two Egypts: one was inhabited by a wealthy military and civilian elite that lived in gated communities; the other was an impoverished populace that welcomed Muslim Brotherhood-run education and social programs that made up for a failing state system.

USAID officials made mistakes in Egypt, Ward admitted, but the structure of the post–Camp David agreement allowed the Mubarak regime to manipulate the spending of vast amounts of aid.

"There was an entitlement attitude," Ward said, "that this is our money and we will spend it in a way that makes sense to us, and that did not lead to a lot of discussion about serious reform."

Today Egypt's economic challenges are larger and more difficult than those of Tunisia and Libya. Its long-term prospects are bleaker. The country has a sprawling population of 80 million—eight times the size of Tunisia or Libya. The illiteracy rate is 28 percent, and 25 percent of the people live in poverty. Much of the country's economy remains state-run, and since the overthrow of Mubarak it has been in free fall.

GDP fell from a healthy 5.1 percent before the uprising to 1.5 percent afterward, according to the IMF. Foreign direct investment plummeted from $2.1 billion to $218 million. Egypt's foreign currency reserves dropped from $36 billion to about $10 billion. And tourism revenue, one of the country's main sources of foreign currency, slumped 18 percent to $7.1 billion. Most worrisome of all, youth unemployment hovers at about 25 percent, a volatile situation in a country where 80 percent of the population is under thirty.

And in a development that alarms many American and Israeli officials, the Muslim Brotherhood has emerged as the dominant political force in Egypt. After a protracted power struggle with the Egyptian army, Mohammed Morsi, the senior Muslim Brotherhood official who is Egypt's first democratically elected president, removed the senior army officers who tried to limit his power in August 2012.

When this book went to press in December 2012, Morsi and other Brotherhood officials insisted that they will abide by democratic norms, uphold the peace treaty with Israel, and work with the international community to modernize Egypt's economy. But they have also made clear that public opinion in Egypt can no longer be ignored.

"After the revolution, everyone realizes that Egypt's foreign relations are different from those before the revolution," Essam El Erian, an adviser to Morsi and a senior Brotherhood official, said in September. "Now the citizenry is watching closely and the elected president must take popular sentiment into consideration, and keep elections in mind. The U.S. president is also doing this; all elected presidents are mindful of the public will."

One of the largest challenges facing the Obama administration in its second term is how to deal with the Brotherhood and its newfound power. As long as it continues to abide by democratic and international norms, I believe its right to rule Egypt should be respected. Founded in 1928, the Islamist political movement endured decades of brutal crackdowns by the Egyptian military. In the 1970s, it renounced violence, embraced elections, and began launching vast social service programs to aid Egypt's poor. The AKP party in Turkey, Ennahda in Tunisia, and Hamas in Palestine all model themselves after the Brotherhood. Today it has enormous sway with conservative Muslims across the Middle East. It represents both an opportunity and a danger to the United States.

Ward called for the United States to listen to Egypt's new leaders and not repeat the mistakes of the post–Camp David era.

"I think the best way to show the new government that we do want to help is to adopt the tactic we used in Libya: listen," Ward said. "Really engage them in a dialogue about what their needs are and build some trust."

The signing of the 1978 Camp David Accords was a diplomatic triumph for the Carter administration and an economic boon for Israel and Egypt. As part of the Accords, Congress passed laws mandating billions of dollars in annual foreign aid to Egypt and Israel. For the next twenty years, Israel and Egypt were the largest recipients of American foreign aid in the world, receiving more than 50 percent of the entire American foreign aid budget. Throughout the 1980s and 1990s, Israel received $3 billion in annual military aid and grants and Egypt received $1.5 billion in annual military aid and $815 million in civilian aid. For all other countries, foreign aid was set on a yearly basis and fluctuated wildly, a practice that development experts said made effective projects impossible.

Ward first arrived in Cairo in 1988. Two years earlier, he had joined USAID after graduating from the School of Law at the University of California, Berkeley, and working as a lawyer in Washington for four years. At that time, the annual tranches of $815 million in civilian aid went to infrastructure, health, and agricultural development projects, he said. Using American construction firms, USAID built a modern phone system and the sewage and water systems in Cairo and Alexandria.

"It was huge," Ward recalled. "There were 105 Foreign Service officers with AID alone in Cairo. I was the second Mark Ward working for AID, which got very confusing."

The Soviet Union's $1 billion construction of the Aswan High Dam in the 1960s had set a new standard in the cold war competition between Moscow and Washington to win hearts and minds in the Middle East. In a seeming coup for the Soviets, the completion of the massive dam in 1970 ended centuries of flooding by the Nile and helped modernize Egyptian agriculture. Critics of USAID said the agency had created no comparable high-profile post–Camp David American project in Egypt. But USAID experts said massive infrastructure projects—particularly dams—were wasteful, ineffective, and bad development.

The debate resurrected an unresolved core question inside the U.S. government. Is the purpose of American civilian aid programs to help the United States government achieve its political goals in other parts of the world? Or should these efforts be purely humanitarian?

The debate remains unresolved and handicaps American efforts in other countries as well. In Afghanistan and Pakistan, senior officials in the Bush and Obama administrations favored large, high-visibility infrastructure projects. USAID staffers resisted the ideas and argued that they were poor development practice.

"There is just a complete lack of what the broader vision is," said a senior State Department official who is critical of USAID, "what the broader political goals are."

Frustrated members of Congress passed laws that created their own aid programs, some of which were clearly about currying favor with their own constituents, not aiding Egyptians. From 1986 to 2008, the congressionally created Commodity Import Program provided hundreds of millions of dollars in financing to Egyptian companies to buy U.S. goods and sell them to Egypt. The project was called development but it clearly benefited American companies.

Too weak to determine its own direction but too large to be completely eliminated, USAID has long been used by various entities in Washington to achieve their own short-term agendas. It has also been the subject of ridicule on Capitol Hill or in the media. In the 1990s, Senator Jesse Helms of North Carolina famously accused the agency of pouring American taxpayer dollars down "foreign rat holes." In truth, the agency's primary purpose during that decade was shoveling congressionally mandated cash to Egypt.

In 1999, the Clinton administration reduced civilian aid to Egypt to $600 million while continuing to provide $1.5 billion a year to the Egyptian military. George W. Bush continued the reductions. By 2008, civilian aid had dropped to $411 million.

At the same time, members of the Bush administration and Congress began demanding more aggressively that the reduced American aid be used to fund democracy and human rights organizations in Egypt.

The Mubarak regime bitterly resisted having American aid flow to prodemocracy groups, and tried to redirect it to communities that the government deemed loyal.

When the Obama administration took office in 2009, it cut civilian aid even further, from $410 million to $250 million a year. And in an apparent effort to reduce tensions with the Mubarak government, the administration cut funding to NGOs in Egypt to roughly $25 million.

After the president's speech in Cairo, the administration launched the Partners for a New Beginning program, which brought the delegation of American high-tech entrepreneurs to Tunis, and a similar initiative called the Global Entrepreneurship Program, as well as several small-scale programs to foster science and technical cooperation. The Overseas Private Investment Corporation created a $100 million enterprise fund for small businesses in the Middle East and North Africa. And in December 2010, the administration launched an initiative to encourage cooperation between Egyptian and American scientists.

A month later, Egyptian protesters gathered in Tahrir Square for the first time. Instead of simplifying U.S. civilian efforts, the revolution would complicate them.

As the protests in Tahrir reached a critical mass in January 2011, Obama tried to strike a middle ground. In carefully constructed statements from Washington, he urged the Mubarak government to respect protesters' right to free speech and called for peaceful demonstrations.

In Cairo, Obama's careful stance backfired. His cautious response to the protests confirmed Egyptians' suspicions that the United States was continuing to support Mubarak. Obama eventually helped force Mubarak from power, but his popularity dropped in Egypt.

In 2009, Egyptians were split about Obama, with 47 percent saying they did not have confidence in his actions and 42 percent saying they did. In 2012, 69 percent of Egyptians said they did not have confidence in Obama and 29 percent said they did trust his actions.

Meanwhile, Mubarak loyalists and members of the Egyptian military became increasingly convinced that the United States had secretly fomented the antigovernment protests. As I had seen across the region, Washington was still perceived as an all-powerful force, despite its debacles in Iraq and Afghanistan.

Ten months after Mubarak was forced from power, Egypt's then military rulers took revenge. In December 2011, Egyptian police raided the offices of seventeen foreign nonprofit organizations—including two American ones—that were running democracy promotion programs in Egypt. They confiscated money, computers, and files, and shut down their operations. When outraged American officials threatened to withhold American civilian aid, Egyptian military authorities upped the stakes. In February 2012, they announced that forty-three people who worked for the organizations, including nineteen Americans, would be put on trial for operating illegally in Egypt.

Both of the American-financed groups—the National Democratic Institute and the International Republican Institute—had been chartered by Congress to promote democracy abroad through election monitoring and running nonpartisan workshops on political organizing. One of the Americans facing charges was Sam LaHood, director of the Republican Institute's Egypt office and the son of Ray LaHood, a former Republican congressman from Illinois and the Obama administration's transportation secretary.

Outraged members of Congress called for the administration to withhold its $250 million in civilian aid, and the $1.5 billion in military aid as well. After several weeks, Egypt's military rulers backed down. In March, the Americans were allowed to leave the country after posting nearly $5 million in bail money. Several days later, Clinton formally approved the release of the $1.5 billion in military aid to Egypt.

Apparently emboldened after its confrontation with the Americans, the Egyptian army next attacked the Muslim Brotherhood. In parliamentary elections in late 2011, the Brotherhood had won 37 percent of the vote and hard-line Salafist parties had come in second with 28 percent. In a result that shocked and unnerved the Egyptian military, and Washington, Islamists from various parties garnered 65 percent of the vote.

As it became increasingly clear that the Brotherhood's candidate would win the country's first post-Mubarak presidential election in June 2012, the military tried to cling to power. The ruling military council enacted decrees giving it absolute power. Military-backed courts dissolved the country's Islamist-dominated parliament. When the Brotherhood's presidential candidate, Mohammed Morsi, was elected president, no one knew, in fact, who ruled the country.

When Hillary Clinton visited Cairo three weeks later, Egypt's extremists emerged. She saw both its peril and its promise. As she exited the recently reopened American consulate in Alexandria, pro-Mubarak demonstrators hurled shoes and tomatoes at her car, shouted "Monica," and accused her of fixing Egypt's presidential elections so that the Brotherhood would win.

Clinton then visited Flat6Labs, a high-tech incubator in Cairo that provides money and support to young entrepreneurs. The two-year-old "start-up accelerator" had received hundreds of applications for twenty spots in a six-month incubation program.

In a subsequent interiew, the chairman of the Flat6Labs, Ahmed El Alfi, told journalist Lauren Bohn that most of the budding entrepreneurs who seek Flat6Labs' mentoring are public-school-educated and from a lower economic bracket.

"These are the people who can't just pack up and move to the West," Alfi said. "The revolution gave people a sense of empowerment."

Three-quarters of Egypt's 80 million people live outside Cairo in rural areas that receive little media attention and inhabit a world disconnected from the televised revolution that was Tahrir Square. Over time, rural Egypt will show the true reach of the revolution—and its limits.

"Instead of calling up your dad to call up his friends to get you a government job, now Egyptians are thinking outside of the box; they want to make a difference," Alfi told Bohn. "We have to nurture this talent, support creativity, and harness the power as an economic solution."

But he and many others fear that continued instability may prompt a brain drain among the brightest of Egypt's elite.

Four Egyptians from Upper Egypt, the country's impoverished hinterlands, submitted one of the winning business proposals. They proposed creating an Egyptian version of Etsy, the American Web site that showcases and sells the work of independent artists and artisans. The Egyptian site will showcase the work of artisans across Egypt and simultaneously tell the story of their lives.

Their goal is twofold: First, to create a compelling, personal product and dismantle stereotypes about average Egyptians held by both foreigners and Cairo's moneyed elite. Second, to use e-commerce to preserve Egypt's traditional handcraft sector, which still makes up a large proportion of the country's labor force but faces an uncertain future in the face of modernization and globalization.

"This project is about enabling producers' direct access to markets," Usama Mohammed, one of the project's founders, told Bohn. "A whole swath of Egypt doesn't have any access, and opportunities are lessening due to their lack of IT and business skills. We need to empower these nontraditional markets."

One major Egyptian player is Ziad Mokhtar, a principal at Ideavelopers, the venture capital arm of Cairo-based EFG-Hermes, one of the Middle East's leading investment banks. Ideavelopers manages a $50 million fund focused on technology start-ups. Mokhtar is in charge of finding new investment opportunities in the region but is worried by the lack of major investments by Western tech companies in the Arab world. The only major buyout was Yahoo!'s acquisition of the Jordanian Web site Maktoob for an estimated $85 million in 2009.

"We have a lot of enthusiastic entrepreneurs now," Mokhtar told Bohn. "But my worry is—will this enthusiasm last? Is this entrepreneurship buzz just a bubble, just hype? Will investors ultimately come into the country and buy these companies? I'm not sure. We haven't really seen any big buys in the Middle East. So that's a big, potentially worrying question mark."

Egyptians point out that while there is not even a word for *entrepreneurship* in Arabic, the number of incubators keeps growing. Along with Flat6Labs and an incubator named Tahrir Square, Vodafone—one of Egypt's largest mobile phone companies—is launching an "incubator arm" of its own.

Young, tech-savvy Egyptians warn that Egyptians who are not members of the country's 1 percent don't see "entrepreneurship" as a viable route.

"We're always taught to be an engineer, a doctor," Sabrine Assem, a young woman working on a start-up at Flat6Labs, told Bohn. "Those are solid, steady jobs. What is entrepreneurship? Most Egyptians can't even say the word."

USAID thinks the answer may be an Egyptian version of *The Apprentice.* The agency is trying to transfer a successful television program it funded in Afghanistan to Egypt, according to *Fast Company* magazine. In 2010, a twenty-seven-year-old American named Anna Elliot launched a reality TV show in Afghanistan called *Dream and Achieve.* An Afghan version of *The Apprentice,* the show pitted Afghan men and women with business ideas against one another. Audience members chose the winner.

One contestant, an ex–military commander hoping to run a dairy farm with his soldiers, was quickly voted off the program. A female contestant hoped to start a jam-and-pickle company that employed widows and refugees. When the Taliban found out she was on the show, the woman was forced to move out of her hometown. The eventual winner was a man who used the program's twenty-thousand-dollar prize to start a plastic recycling plant that would run on renewable energy. The show's finale drew 7 million viewers, making it the top-rated show of the season in Afghanistan.

David Elliot, Anna Elliot's father, told Bohn they hoped the Egyptian version of the program would reach an audience beyond the country's 1 percent.

"We want these young, spirited, talented Egyptians who want to do something," he said, "who want to make something of themselves, to say, 'I want to be an entrepreneur.'"

Habib Haddad, a self-described "serial entrepreneur," said he was betting on the Egyptian diaspora. Haddad is the CEO of Wamda, a platform designed to empower entrepreneurs in the region with a media site, funding, and programming. Haddad said Egyptians living or studying abroad were coming back to Egypt to work and innovate instead of staying in California or New York.

One example was Negma, a group established by seven Egyptian American and Egyptian professionals from the Harvard and MIT communities. The group had received scores of proposals for call centers, youth groups, and green technology companies that would have positive economic or social impacts in Egypt. Its members planned to provide funding and mentoring to the most promising projects. In its first competition, the group decided to fund an Egyptian American graduate of Georgetown University who hoped to create an Egyptian version of the Teach for America program.

Hovering over all the projects, though, was the question of scale, reform, and sustainability. If Egypt failed to enact economic reform, stabilize politically, or attract a vast amount of foreign investment, broad economic growth would not occur. Incubators, reality shows, and talk of entrepreneurship would not be enough.

In many ways, Egypt's biggest challenge is its education system. A 2012 Chatham House paper by Louisa Loveluck laid out the scope of the problems. Thirty-two percent of Egyptians are under the age of fifteen. Unless its schools and universities are radically reformed, the next generation of Egyptian youth will be a source of instability for decades to come.

The imbalance between the skills of graduates of Egypt's education system and the needs of its employers has created a consistently high unemployment rate, according to Chatham House. The country's official unemployment rate is 12 percent, but it is widely believed to be far higher. Among Egyptians under twenty-five and university graduates, unemployment is particularly high.

On average, it takes Egyptian university graduates five years to find a job, according to a regional NGO, Injaz Al-Arab. The country's anemic education system creates a two-tiered society that exacerbates social tensions. While the poor attend decrepit public schools, the rich send their children to expensive private schools and universities that give them vast advantages in education and skills. Sweeping economic inequality results.

Egypt's education system has long been manipulated by its rulers. Under Ottoman rule in the early nineteenth century, a European educational system was introduced to "nurture a class of well-educated, loyal administrators and army officers who would become the national army," according to Chatham House. During British rule from 1882 to 1922, investment in public education was slashed in an effort to reduce the risk of educated, nationalist leaders emerging to challenge colonial rule.

After Egypt gained independence, President Gamel Abdel

Nasser made education a central part of his famed pan-Arabist modernizing project. Nasser gradually made education free for all Egyptians—from elementary schools to universities—and Egyptian-trained teachers fanned out across the region, bringing with them an Egyptian curriculum that influenced schools throughout the Middle East, according to Chatham House.

In a final step that proved disastrous, Nasser guaranteed that all university graduates would be hired as government workers. Enrollments soared, poorly trained professors were hired to meet the demand, and the quality of higher education plummeted.

Overcrowding became endemic as well, particularly in urban areas, and schools began to operate in shifts, Chatham House said. The result today is disastrously high teacher-student ratios—often around one to fifty in poor urban areas—and widespread gender inequality.

On average in Egyptian schools, the number of female students is 20 percent lower than the number of males, and girls drop out more often than boys. Progress has been made in raising the female literacy rate. Today 63 percent of Egyptian women are literate. Among men, 80 percent are literate.

In overcrowded public schools, students often cram on benches, sharing desk space. Laboratories, playgrounds, and music and art rooms are rare, according to Egyptian education experts. Classes focus on rote learning, and advancement depends on results of standardized tests, not critical thinking.

A final element that cements the ossified system in place is the low pay and social status of teachers, who earn $281 a month on average, according to Chatham House. Desperate parents have turned to private tutoring to make up for the low quality of public schools. Today private tutoring accounts for 60 percent of education spending in Egypt, according to the country's Central Agency for Public Mobilization and Statistics.

Private tutoring has become so widespread that it has created an incentive for teachers to not finish their lesson plans, the Chatham House paper said. After school, many teachers work as private tutors and offer to complete their lessons in exchange for cash.

Egyptian writer Tarek Osman told Bohn that shifting the education system from rote learning to critical thinking was vital for the country's economy and stability.

"The fundamental drive should be toward developing the thinking of the young: critical reasoning, information assessment, deduction," said Osman. "The kind of skills that seriously matter in fast-changing economies."

Egypt's elite American University in Cairo costs twenty thousand dollars a year and is home to what Egyptians call the "Gucci Corner," an area where well-off students lounge in designer clothes. At the country's other extreme, public universities cost twenty dollars per year.

Employers say it is difficult to find recruits with adequate training in both sector-specific skills and the "soft skills" needed by business, from problem solving to time management. Malak Zaalouk, a professor at the American University in Cairo and former UNICEF regional senior education adviser in Egypt, called for American officials to wait for the country's new government to develop its education policies and then support them. She said that forcing American projects onto the Egyptians will be premature, wasteful, and resented. "What's really important is that the country has a plan and vision," she said. "An aid environment and aid mechanisms should fit into a vision and plan. At this current time, we don't have that. So, we're talking about aid potentially being poured into a dark alley. There's no accountability. Nothing is clear."

Khaled Gamal represents an Egypt far from start-up incubators—poor young men who don't have time to protest because they are too busy working. Since his father died when he was ten, Gamal, eighteen, has worked in a tin shop or as a construction laborer in one of Cairo's poorest neighborhoods, Manshiyat Nasr.

In a June 2012 interview with journalist Lauren Bohn, Gamal said he someday hopes to be an engineer. Echoing the sentiments of many of his friends, Gamal knew he could not "become an adult" until he made enough money to support himself—and a potential bride.

Unemployment and soaring living costs have created a marriage crisis in Egypt. In Egyptian culture, men must provide their wives with an apartment, but for many young men that is increasingly difficult. Some analysts describe Egypt's marriage crisis as a social time bomb created by the postponement of many disenfranchised Egyptian youths' passage into adulthood.

"I'm proud of the life I live, but it's the type of life that had us in Tahrir the first few days fighting for a better one," he said. "I want a better sewage system, a good high school. The poor are constantly forgotten by the regime and even the revolutionaries."

He said only well-connected Egyptians could thrive.

"Unless you're the son or daughter of well-known people, or unless you know someone high up, you can't get anything done and you definitely can't move up," he told Bohn. "The system has always been and still is the rule of connections."

Ward said it is clear what Egypt needs more than anything else: jobs. He said the best way for the United States to help Egypt's government create jobs would be to encourage foreign and domestic private investment. Promoting transparency in the Egyptian government and improving the education and training of Egyptian workers would help as well.

"If you get the accountability and the transparency right, you're going to have investment by major companies, foreign and domestic," he said. "And if the training comes together, those new employers are going to find the workers they need close at hand."

There is a desperate need for an American civilian aid approach in Egypt that is more effective than the post–Camp David effort. Egypt can end up like Pakistan, an unstable rump democracy dominated by a kleptocratic and paranoid military. Or Egypt can follow the path of Turkey.

It is vital that the United States waits and listens in Egypt. Washington faces an extraordinary public policy conundrum there. Decades of support for Mubarak will not be forgotten overnight.

On his first trip to the United States as Egypt's democratically elected president, Morsi attended the United Nations General Assembly in September 2012. In speeches at the UN and the Clinton Global Initiative, Morsi conveyed the mix of fierce independence, sense of grievance, and desire to be a respected part of the world community that dominates Egypt today.

He urged American businesses to invest in Egypt and said he was uninterested in loans. He insisted that Islam, capitalism, democracy, and minority rights were all compatible. He called for new laws to be enacted in the United States that would make the amateur anti-Muslim video hate speech. And he asked for respect of Egyptian and Islamic culture.

"The world cannot become one culture or one civilization," he said at the Clinton Global Initiative. "However, can we have civilizations that live side by side, not against one another? It is possible."

And he urged American tourists to return to the country, recognizing how vital they are to Egypt's economy. "You are all invited to come to see the new Egypt," he said. "We have a new democratic state, a new civil state. It's not a theocratic state. It's not secular. It's not military."

* * *

More than any other country, Egypt represents an opportunity for the United States to break old paradigms in the Middle East, create new alliances, and isolate Salafists. If the Muslim Brotherhood continues to reject violence, abide by democratic norms, and embrace international human rights, it should not be considered an enemy of the United States.

If Egypt backs Hamas and other militant groups militarily or financially, it should be considered an enemy of Israel. But if it pursues a diplomatic resolution to the Israeli-Palestinian conflict and maintains Egypt's peace treaty with Israel, it should not.

Egypt has a right to demand an end to the Israeli-Palestinian conflict. The Brotherhood is likely to be bellicose about Israel and decry Israeli attacks on Gaza. But statements are different from supporting violent attacks.

More than anything, the United States must think strategically in Egypt, be patient, and engage in nonmilitary ways. As Chris Stevens did in Libya, American officials should listen patiently as Egypt finds its way. Panicking, being overly aggressive, or trying to force Western models on Egypt will backfire.

If Egyptians request assistance, American officials should discuss using the European Union accession program that was applied to Turkey. Washington could create a series of generous incentives for economic reforms in Egypt but allow Egyptian officials to decide whether or not to implement them. It should encourage the same type of foreign investment in Egypt that revitalized Turkey.

Backing an anti-Islamist coup by the Egyptian military would be a disaster that would fuel fundamentalism in Egypt and the region. Washington should listen to Egyptians and hold its nerve as Egypt finds its way. After decades of American-backed Mubarak rule, most Egyptians see America as its enemy. We must not forget that.

CHAPTER 9

Little Washington

As millions of Egyptians watched President Obama's Cairo address in June 2009, Steven R. Koltai, a fifty-five-year-old former Warner Brothers executive and Internet entrepreneur, watched the speech from his vacation home in Maine. Obama's vow to host a Summit on Entrepreneurship between American and Muslim business leaders surprised, thrilled, and inspired him.

The State Department had recently accepted Koltai as a Franklin Fellow, a new Obama administration initiative designed to bring private sector and academic experts to work at the State Department and USAID for a year. On paper, the program was an innovative attempt to help the government marshal the expertise of American business and academia. But it was so poorly funded that it served instead as yet another example of the debilitated state of federal civilian agencies.

The fellowship was unpaid and did not offer fellows a housing stipend. Instead, the State Department asked that businesses and academic institutions pay fellows salaries during their year in Washington. After thirty years in the private sector, Koltai was wealthy enough that he didn't need a salary, but he was deeply skeptical of government in general. Obama's embrace of entrepreneurship, though, convinced him to accept the fellowship.

"This is my life's work," Koltai later said, referring to promoting entrepreneurship. "The United States has not put what I consider the central strand of our DNA into the service of our foreign policy."

Bald, bearish, and intensely driven, Koltai was born in Hungary. He and his family fled the country when he was a toddler during the 1956 Hungarian Revolution. The child of an academic, he grew up in Los Angeles and Kansas City, Missouri, and received a bachelor's degree from Tufts University in 1976 and a master's degree from Tuft's Fletcher School of Law and Diplomacy in 1978.

Most of his classmates chose to become diplomats and bankers. Koltai, a fluent Hungarian and French speaker, became a businessman and consultant with a blue-chip résumé. In the 1980s, he worked at McKinsey & Company, Salomon Brothers, and cofounded a firm that would become SES/Astra, one of Europe's largest satellite television companies. Returning to Los Angeles in 1987, he married, had two sons, and worked as a senior executive at Warner Brothers for nine years.

In the late 1990s, he rode the tech bubble—and bust. In 1996, Koltai founded Event411, an online event registration and management company that provided the software for the 2000 Los Angeles Democratic National Convention, the 2000 Salt Lake City Winter Olympics, and corporate clients. After the dot-com bubble burst and the 9/11 attacks decimated the convention business, the firm went out of business in 2002.

Since then, Koltai has run his own consulting and investment company, advising Lifetime Television, serving on various boards at Tufts, and helping the school develop an entrepreneurial leadership program. In August 2009, he arrived for his first day of work at the

State Department. His time in Washington would change his opinion of government forever.

From his first day, Koltai hurled himself into turning Obama's promise of hosting a summit for entrepreneurs into reality. His mentor and boss was Lorraine Hariton, the State Department's special representative for commercial and business affairs. A successful Silicon Valley executive, Hariton, like Richard Holbrooke, was one of a handful of "special representatives" Clinton had appointed to address the country's most pressing foreign policy issues—Afghanistan-Pakistan, Israel-Palestine, and dismally low American exports.

Hariton and Koltai believed that promoting entrepreneurship would spark economic development, foster political stability, create jobs, and strengthen civil society in predominantly Muslim communities. Koltai spent his first three months as the lead organizer of Obama's promised Presidential Summit on Entrepreneurship. Held in April 2010, it brought 220 entrepreneurs from 55 Muslim communities to Washington.

Koltai then helped launch the Global Entrepreneurship Program, a seemingly model public-private partnership that included Cisco, Ernst & Young, and Google from the private sector; MIT, Babson College, and the American University in Cairo from academia; and Endeavor and TechnoServ from the nonprofit world. USAID, the Overseas Private Investment Corporation, the Small Business Administration, and the Commerce Department participated as well.

The program opened offices in Egypt, Indonesia, and Turkey, where "lead entrepreneurs" operated programs that gave local entrepreneurs mentoring, training, and contact with American angel investors. Koltai and others led "entrepreneurship delegations" that brought successful start-up executives, angel investors, and business school professors to Lebanon, Jordan, Egypt, and Indonesia.

Koltai was incensed by the lack of financial support for the program. He managed to temporarily cobble together $1.5 million from various initiatives but never secured permanent funding—or staffers—for it. Every single one of the entrepreneurs and venture capitalists he invited to the region were forced to pay for their own airfares.

"The kind of program I'm talking about—for the world, it's $100 million," he said. "It is a rounding error."

Members of Congress were happy to hurl money at the Defense Department but skeptical about increasing the size of the State Department for any reason. And State Department officials were more interested in traditional diplomacy.

Koltai found government workers underpaid, cautious, and cynical. They "yawned" at the announcement of new presidential initiatives, according to Koltai, dismissing the programs as political theatrics or changes that the next administration would reverse in four years. Instead of rushing to carry out the president's orders, some State Department staffers did just enough to not endanger their jobs. Others, he found, were committed to government service but beaten down by a system that resisted changed.

"There are an incredible number of really smart, really dedicated people who are incredibly frustrated," he said.

Fearful of criticism and budget cuts from Capitol Hill, risk aversion was endemic across the government, according to Koltai and other former government officials who had worked in the private sector. In business, taking risks and failing was expected. In government, members of Congress and the news media lampooned the smallest mistake.

"I was able to generate zero dollars of funding and zero FTEs," Koltai said, using the term for full-time-equivalent employees. "What we were able to do was write speeches."

One midlevel administration official who worked in the venture capital field before taking a post in the Obama administration said the public system was paralyzed. In venture capital, he said, as many as eighteen out of twenty investments lose money, but the goal is to learn from one's mistakes. In Washington, a single failure can doom a career.

"It's very hard to innovate and to learn in these programs," said the official, who asked not to be named. "If you fail once, you get screwed." The result was an extraordinarily cautious and territorial system that infuriated Koltai. Government workers, meanwhile, found him grating.

"He was a one-man show," recalled a government official who worked with Koltai and also asked not to be named. "To succeed in Washington, you have to be a team player and bring people along with you."

What angered Koltai the most was the government's reliance on contractors. While government bureaucrats fretted over evaporating slots, funding, and authority, contractors overflowed with resources. As a business executive, Koltai was astonished by how the contracting system worked.

Based on the numbers he saw while in government and his own experience running businesses, he estimated that State Department contractors regularly made a 30 percent profit while performing poorly and facing little competition. He watched cautious and overworked government contracting officers choose the same firm year after year because doing so allowed them to avoid congressional or media scrutiny.

"The only way to not make a mistake is to do nothing," Koltai said. "And the only way to not choose the wrong contractor is to choose the one you're already using."

After the fall of Mubarak, Koltai tried to convince USAID to revamp a $34 million program that had been created in 2008 to "improve the business environment" in Egypt. With more freedom to operate in the country, he hoped to divert some of the money to training young Egyptian technology entrepreneurs and exposing them to American executives and investors.

But the contractor—Chemonics—the same company that had hired Chuck Grader years earlier in southern Afghanistan—refused to change the program. When the USAID procurement officer handling the contract challenged Chemonics, he found himself outnumbered. Citing language in its contract, the company threatened to go to court over the issue. The system astounded Koltai.

"Chemonics has a whole legal department whose existence is based on memorizing the fine print," he said. "The person overseeing the public money is outgunned. We, the American taxpayer, did not have the right to say 'stop the presses, there's been a revolution.'"

The USAID procurement officer impressed him. He declined to name him but said he was a "smart, dedicated" civil servant, with relatively low pay, scant support, and tough working conditions.

"He was paid eighty-five thousand dollars while managing hundreds of thousands of dollars," Koltai said. "You'd never find that in the private sector."

After his one-year fellowship ended, he was hired by the State Department to continue on as a senior adviser for entrepreneurship. After two years, he left in frustration. The depth of Washington's polarization depressed Koltai. Business was not inherently evil, as the Far Left contended. And government was not inherently a menace, as the Far Right contended. Koltai believed that Silicon Valley and other successful entrepreneurial "ecosystems" were the product of public and private partnerships. Together, federally funded research universities and ruthlessly capitalistic venture capital firms created innovation.

"There is no example of a successful entrepreneurial system that did not have the government in the lead," Koltai said. "You don't just start a venture fund. You don't just do training. You do a basket of things."

But implementing new initiatives proved extraordinarily difficult. The byzantine federal procurement process minimized risk—the opposite of the venture capital system—and blocked change.

"The number one problem in connecting the dots is the procurement process," he said. "In my view, the key to changing that is on the Hill."

Until the president and Congress revamp civilian agencies, implementing dynamic policies will be difficult.

"If the axle of the car is broken," he said, "whether Mario Andretti or you gets behind the wheel, you're not going to be able to drive it."

The decay in civilian agencies is part of a broad, long-term shift of money, talent, and authority from the public sector to the private sector that began with the Reagan, Bush, and Clinton administrations. And as the contracting business exploded in Washington during the 1990s and 2000s, Wall Street firms—smelling a profit—arrived in force.

Well before other venture capital firms, the Carlyle Group successfully rode the contracting wave. In 1989, David M. Rubenstein, a lawyer and former domestic policy adviser to President Jimmy Carter, cofounded the firm with William E. Conway Jr., a former MCI executive, and Daniel A. D'Aniello, a corporate executive. Over the course of the 1990s, Carlyle bought up defense and aerospace companies and quickly became the leading private equity investor in the sector.

The driving force behind the strategy was Frank Carlucci, a former Reagan administration national security adviser and defense secretary. A college roommate of Donald Rumsfeld at Princeton and former CIA operative, Carlucci served as the Carlyle Group's chairman from 1992 to 2003.

James Baker III, former secretary of state, served as the group's senior counselor, and its advisers and executives included former President George H. W. Bush, former Clinton White House Chief of Staff Thomas "Mack" McLarty, former Securities and Exchange Commission Chairman Arthur Levitt, former British Prime Minister John Major, and former Philippines President Fidel Ramos. A half-brother of Osama bin Laden who was estranged from the al-Qaeda leader invested in Carlyle in the 1990s. He withdrew the funds after the 9/11 attacks.

Carlyle profited from the invasions of Afghanistan and Iraq by cashing out at the right time. Its largest defense investment was the 1997 purchase of United Defense Industries—which makes artillery, missiles, and other weapons systems. As the Iraq war raged in 2004, Carlyle sold the company to the British defense conglomerate BAE at a profit of $1 billion. In 2008, Carlyle purchased government contractor Booz Allen Hamilton for $2.5 billion. In 2012, Booz Allen received $3.8 billion in federal contracts, much of it for work with the CIA, and was the eighth-largest federal contractor.

Today Carlyle is legendary in private equity circles. Company officials say they buy poorly managed firms, revamp them, and provide better services to the government and consumers. It has $150 billion in assets, invests across the economy, and owns companies ranging from Bain Capital to Dunkin' Donuts. The firm's three founders are believed to be worth as much as $2 billion each.

DynCorp, meanwhile, continues to grow. In 2012, it was the tenth-largest government contractor in the country and received $3.8 billion in federal contracts. As of November 2012, the company's current owner remains Cerberus Capital Management, the $20 billion New York–based private equity firm headed by longtime Republican donor Stephen Feinberg. Cerberus's senior executives include former Vice President Dan Quayle and former Bush administration Treasury Secretary John Snow.

Another firm with Wall Street ties that profited handsomely while performing questionably as a contractor is BearingPoint, the global consulting firm that was hired to provide training and monitoring to the Afghan Ministry of Finance. Between 2001 and 2009, the McLean, Virginia–based firm received $1 billion in State Department contracts to work in the Afghan and Iraqi finance ministries. Auditors later found that the firm failed to report signs of the looting of up to $850 million from Afghanistan's Kabul Bank to U.S. officials. After expanding too quickly around the world, Bearing-Point filed for bankruptcy in 2009.

New York–based Deloitte, the Wall Street professional services firm, bought BearingPoint's government contracting business and took over its Afghanistan operation. Auditors found that Deloitte also failed to report to U.S. officials signs that Kabul Bank was being looted. Officials from Deloitte said the firm's work in Afghanistan was "primarily advisory" and "included assistance with training programs and advising on rules and procedures" but did not involve "supervision or examination of any bank." The firm continues to receive work from the U.S. government. In fiscal 2011, Deloitte won $1.1 billion in federal contractors and was the twenty-seventh-largest government contractor in the United States.

Chemonics, the firm whose conduct in southern Afghanistan angered Chuck Grader nearly a decade ago and Steven Koltai in Egypt more recently, remains on the government payroll. Company officials continue to defend the quality of their work.

In 2006, Scott Spangler, the Republican donor and former Bush administration official who purchased Chemonics in 1999, sold his controlling interest in the firm to Eyk Van Otterloo, a founding partner of Grantham, Mayo, and Van Otterloo & Company, a Boston-based private equity firm with $104 billion in assets. In 2011, Chemonics became employee-owned but Van Otterloo remained chairman. In 2012, the firm was the forty-fifth-largest contractor in the United States. That year, it received $554 million in government contracts, nearly all of them from USAID. It still holds the USAID contract in Egypt, which is both vital and expected to rapidly expand.

USAID, meanwhile, continues to flounder. Between 2001 and 2010, Congress doubled the agency's budget but cut staffing by 30 percent. Some staff was added by the Obama administration, but State, White House, and congressional officials continued to lambaste its performance.

In an effort to remake its image, USAID hired Maura O'Neill as its chief innovation officer in 2010. Before serving as chief of staff for the Agriculture Department and Washington Senator Maria Cantwell, O'Neill started four companies and taught entrepreneurship at the Haas School of Business at the University of California, Berkeley. At USAID, she launched Development Innovation Ventures, a program in which the agency tries to replicate the success of the venture capital model—where the majority of investments fail—and apply it to government. Under the program, USAID invests small amounts in projects—usually less than $1 million—and quickly tests to see whether they succeed or fail. If they succeed, they are scaled up and shifted to other parts of the agency.

"Allow us to make a lot of small investments, fail fast, and scale up what works," she said in an interview.

She argued that the rise of developing economies, from China to Brazil—as well as a surge in technological advances—makes successful development more possible than ever. She and other USAID officials point to the growth of mobile phone use worldwide as an example of technology-driven public-private partnerships that AID can promote.

"The developing world is more dynamic than it has ever been," O'Neill said. "Connective technologies have made more opportunities for breakthroughs."

Mark Ward, the longtime AID official who served as its head of procurement from 2006 to 2008, said the core problem was the agency's lack of staff. Congress hurls money at the agency but refuses to give it staff to manage it.

"Given that the number of Foreign Service officers has fallen so precipitously since the Vietnam War—we have one-tenth of the number we had," he said, "we have no choice but to turn to contractors to do the work."

When Ward was the head of procurement, he oversaw sixty to seventy USAID procurement officers who were expected to monitor aid programs worldwide. Under pressure to approve the dispersals of billions of dollars in assistance, Ward and his staff created enormous contracts.

"We have very few people to keep an eye on the contractors, and that naturally has led to fewer and bigger contracts," he said. "I had plenty of money but I didn't have enough people to oversee the awarding of contracts. What do you do? You award fewer contracts. The way to move the money quickly is to award megacontracts to megacontractors."

He said he shared Holbrooke's desire for smaller contracts. While the veteran diplomats were rough on the edges and at times alienated people, he had the right strategy.

"The right approach, the better approach, is bite-sized contracts and grants that are close to the action, that are more flexible, that can't respond to changed approaches," he said. "That's the thing we need."

The solution, he said, is simple.

"It all begins with doing something that is very boring and very Washington," he said. "You need to hire more contracting officers."

Shamila Chaudhary, the young Pakistani American who worked as a State Department and White House aide, resigned from her position at the National Security Council in 2011. After nearly a decade at the State Department, and the White House, she questioned Washington's commitment to long-term policies in Afghanistan and Pakistan.

"When I left I was depressed and disappointed," she said. "I was depressed because I didn't really see an end in sight. I didn't see how we were going to improve the relations we had with both of these countries based on the timeline we had, which was very short."

She said she disagreed with some of Koltai's criticisms. The government will always function differently from the private sector, she said, because taxpayers' dollars are at stake. In the government, numerous stakeholders must be brought on board to win approval of new initiatives. In the private sector, a limited number of major investors are involved.

"The number of people you are accountable to is much less, that's why you get things done much faster," she said. "In the government, you are accountable to every American citizen. These are taxpayer dollars and people take that very seriously."

Chaudhary described the process of drafting new policies, building support for them, and implementing them as arduous.

"You have to build consensus and political will at so many levels," she said. "And when you do that you usually get something that is very watered down, something that is not really as ambitious as the first person thought."

She said the core problem was that American officials were unable to move beyond seeing Afghanistan and Pakistan as security threats to the United States, not nations. She wished a more long-term, normalized relationship could exist.

"When you actually talked about it in nonsecurity ways, people couldn't get their heads around it," she said. "It's not Pakistan for Pakistan's sake. It's not Afghanistan for Afghanistan's sake."

For understandable reasons, even though it is counterproductive in some ways, American policy makers continue to view the region through a counterterrorism prism.

"We're not able to pull ourselves out of this," she said, "because the wounds of 9/11 are still very strong."

Experts point to other dynamics. They argue that the White House and the federal government as a whole lack the ability to identify future threats, try to preempt them, or develop plans to counter them strategically. Micah Zenko, a fellow at the Council on Foreign Relations, argues that the National Security staff needs a separate office that is able to look at long-term strategy and avoid the churn of events. He and other experts point to the strategic planning that the U.S. military carries out as an example. They argue that the National Security staff—or another civilian entity—should be able to engage that same type of long-term planning.

Finally, other observers argue that years of weak funding to the State Department and generous funding to the Pentagon has increased infighting between the two agencies. State Department officials were increasingly turf-conscious. And having a weak State Department created another danger. If Washington does not have organizations that stand up for diplomatic solutions, you are more likely to have military solutions.

Others said the problem was leadership. From the Bush administration's determination to invade Iraq to the Obama administration's desire to get out of Afghanistan, politics and ideology have driven American policy. In administrations, State and Defense department staffers spent months working on policy proposals for the region. The interagency process vetted policies for weeks. In the end, though, Bush's and Obama's senior aides would decide what course of action was best for their president politically.

Politics, of course, have always driven decision making in Washington and always will. But the intensifying partisanship—the worst some observers have seen since World War II—is creating destructive dynamics in Washington.

I do not begrudge the Carlyle Group, DynCorp, or Chemonics. The private sector is doing what it does best: finding innovative ways to make money. The problem is that we have a private sector and military on steroids in the United States. Both are loaded with capital, capacity, and talent. But our public-sector institutions are sclerotic, ossified, and weak.

I do not believe that spending more money or increasing the size of the government is the answer. But we must stop disparaging public service, start paying senior government officials well, and create more dynamic civilian government institutions. Overall, we need a government that is both effective and efficient. Currently, we have neither. For our own national security, that must change.

Conclusion

When this book went to press in December 2012, the murder of Ambassador Stevens and his three colleagues had emerged as a symbol of a dysfunctional civilian effort. An imperfect but functional relationship was emerging between Washington and Egypt's Muslim Brotherhood–led government. And war had not erupted between Israel and Iran.

In Syria, the opposition continued to wage a successful information war against the government. Images of dead civilians whom rebels said had been killed by progovernment forces regularly appeared online. As did images that the opposition might not have wanted to reach a global audience, such as videos showing rebels executing members of a pro-Assad militia. No faction or government in the region seemed able to censor or significantly slow the flow in information, images, and technology.

Moderate leaders in the Syrian opposition, who hoped to model a post-Assad Syria after Turkey, expressed increasing worry about the growing influence of hard-line fundamentalists. Abu Bakr, a Syrian rebel commander interviewed by a Reuters reporter in Syria, said he was a committed Islamist who was determined to overthrow

Assad. But the growing number of radical Muslims who had joined the rebels alarmed him.

"Let me be clear. I am an Islamist, my fighters are Islamists. But there is more than one type of Islamist," he told Reuters. "These men coming fought in insurgencies like Iraq. They are too extreme, they want to blow up any symbol of the state, even schools."

Fighters from Iraq, Saudi Arabia, Kuwait, Libya, eastern Europe, and even the Pakistan-Afghanistan border had joined them in Syria, he and other rebels said. And while they were grateful for the weapons, money, expertise, and determination the jihadists brought, when the war ended they might discover that their jihadist allies had different aims than most Syrians.

"Our goal is to make a new future, not destroy everything," Abu Bakr said. "As bloody as it is now, this stage is simple. We all have the same cause: topple the regime. When Bashar falls, we may find a new battlefront against our former allies."

In Syria and across the post–Arab Spring Middle East, a historic power struggle between moderates and hard-liners will continue for years. Its outcome is of vital importance to the United States, its allies, and the world economy.

In the United States, the focus of the 2012 presidential campaign was understandably jobs, the tepid economy, and the role of government. The killing of Ambassador Stevens in Libya sparked a fierce debate over the Obama administration's initial response but few calls for engagement. American voters, chastened by Iraq, Afghanistan, and an anemic U.S. economy, were uninterested in foreign policy. When it came to the Middle East and Afghanistan, Americans had a clear and consistent message: Get out. Bring the troops home. Stop wasting our funds in a region where we have no allies.

In some ways, they are right. The civilian efforts in Iraq, Afghanistan, and Pakistan were profligate, largely ineffective, and in many ways they even undermined the American efforts they were supposed to support. The owners of contracting companies profited more than American taxpayers, as well as average Iraqis, Afghans, and Pakistanis.

But twenty years of reporting across the Islamic world has convinced me that the United States has allies in the region. The vast majority of Muslims I met were moderates who oppose religious fundamentalism. Yes, they resent American heavy-handedness and what they see as efforts to foist American culture on their countries, but at the same time they resent Salafists who try to forcibly impose an austere form of Islam on them.

In its second term, the core focus of Obama administration policy in the region should be how to quietly, consistently, and effectively support moderates. They are our true allies in the region. Lethal American force alone will not defeat militancy. Local moderates will, by slowly weakening, marginalizing, and discrediting radicalism in the long term.

Whenever possible, American aid should be used to strengthen moderate groups or individuals. From government to businesses to armed forces, the more effective path is to work through local allies and have them engage their societies. They wield far more knowledge, legitimacy, and authority than Americans.

While Americans understandably wish that the United States could divorce itself from the Middle East, that is not realistic. Barring a massive realignment in American politics, Israel's security will continue to be viewed as a vital American interest. For that reason alone, the stability of Egypt and Syria will be considered a priority for Washington. The United States and its European allies also have a vast economic stake in the continued stability of Turkey, Saudi Arabia, and oil-rich Gulf states.

Even as new techniques for extracting oil and natural gas make the United States energy independent, stability in the region will continue to have an enormous impact on global oil prices and the world economy. For decades to come, the economies of China, India, and Europe will remain dependent on Middle Eastern oil. And as an increasingly globalized economy has shown in recent years, an economic shock in Europe or China can derail the American economy.

How, then, can the United States more effectively back these moderates? Each country described in this book presents a different lesson. In Afghanistan's Helmand province, the gutting of American civilian institutions and rise of private contractors produced a profligate and largely ineffective effort. Iraq was an example of ideology and partisanship—the Bush administration's disdain for "Clinton-style nation building"—fueling woeful planning.

The Obama administration's experience in Afghanistan and Pakistan showed that the challenges the United States faces in the region are enormous and not simply the result of incompetent Bush administration policies. The Obama White House revealed how Washington infighting harmed the American effort. And, most important, the Obama surge showed that there are some things the United States simply cannot achieve, even by hurling massive amounts of troops and resources at a problem. The degree of difficulty in changing some local dynamics is simply too high.

Moderates do exist in Afghanistan, Iraq, and Pakistan. The leaders who carried out Afghanistan's remarkably successful health and telecommunications reforms are examples. As are the Iraqi politicians who have tried in vain to bridge the country's sectarian divides. In Pakistan, Monis Rahman, the online entrepreneur, and other members of the country's business elite are eager to trade with India and experience stronger economic growth. In all three countries, fearless human rights advocates, impartial journalists, and smartphone-wielding youth embrace democracy, modernity, and globalism. Afghan President Hamid Karzai, Iraqi Prime Minister Nouri al-Maliki, and Pakistani Army Chief Ashfaq Parvez Kayani should not be viewed as all of Afghanistan, Iraq, and Pakistan.

The United States should stop providing aid to kleptocratic regimes like the Karzai government, militaries like the Pakistani army that suppress democracy, and increasingly authoritarian rulers like al-Maliki. They are unlikely to change. Instead, Washington should reduce its aid in all three countries, take a less central role, and train technocrats, civil society activists, and entrepreneurs over the long term. Helping to create strong middle classes, independent business leaders, and civil society groups has the best chance of gradually promoting stability and moderation.

The central lesson that emerges from America's decade in Afghanistan, Iraq, and Pakistan is that sweeping change is not possible without reliable partners in local governments. Even if the United States perfectly executes its policies and programs, they alone will not stabilize countries. Nations must carry out these reforms themselves. The United States never has been—and never will be—all-powerful. Our hubris and inability to admit our limitations can be one of our enemies.

Traditional American diplomacy should be revived and persistently but quietly pursued. A two-state solution in Israel-Palestine and the easing of India-Pakistan tensions are vital to stabilizing the broader Islamic world. Neither will be achieved quickly, but the United States should quietly and consistently work to resolve these conflicts. We cannot ignore their core roles in sowing tensions.

In Turkey, the Obama administration should more forcefully criticize the antidemocratic excesses of Erdogan. That country can serve as a model for the region only if it is fully democratic. Remaining silent as Turkey's promise is squandered would be tragic for Turkey, the region, and the United States.

In Tunisia, American policy should foster foreign and domestic private investment in the country's high-tech industry, as well as in its traditional textile and auto-manufacturing industries. Tunisia can still be a model of a prosperous post–Arab Spring democracy. Tunisia's Salafists are increasingly bold, but the United States must refrain from any effort to influence the country's internal political debate. Any attempt to do so would backfire, strengthen Salafists, and undermine moderates.

In Libya, Washington must not allow the Benghazi attack to paralyze American diplomacy. The United States should continue Ambassador Stevens's approach, support the new Libyan government's efforts to dissolve militias, and keep Libyans in the lead at all times. Over the long term, creating a viable Libyan government that recognizes the rule of law and a civil society is the best way to honor the memory of Stevens and his colleagues.

In Egypt, the stark lesson is that supporting a military-backed dictator will not work for the long term, no matter how many billions of dollars the United States pours into a country. Embracing generals may look appealing in the short term, but military rule fails to resolve long-term social and economic ills. Working with Egyptians to promote government transparency, foreign and domestic private investment, and education reform are the ways to create Egypt's most vital need: jobs.

A core problem, of course, is Washington. American policy makers must change their antiquated concept of national power. Military might remains vital, but trade with the United States, American technology, and the threat of economic and political isolation are also now powerful national security tools. America's options go beyond military intervention, lethal force, and saber rattling. We must be more savvy, patient, and learned about the existence of potential allies and how to work with them.

Washington's continued infighting and partisanship is taking too great a toll. For six months in 2012, I asked officials across the city to describe the lessons they had learned about the post-9/11 civilian effort. Congressional staffers blamed USAID for the failures. USAID officials blamed Congress. Senior Obama administration officials said government wasn't as dysfunctional as it seemed. One conservative, a former member of the military, said that the country's best and brightest were now in the private sector—and that's where they should be. Washington was divided, tribalized, and angry. No one could agree what the problem was, let alone how to solve it.

As its foreign policy conundrums grow increasingly complex, Washington must be less fractious and more patient. It must reduce its reliance on private contractors and work harder with multilateral organizations and local governments. It should minimize redundancy, join existing bilateral, UN, and World Bank programs where feasible, and focus its aid programs on areas where it has a comparative advantage, such as higher-education reform, short-term energy needs, and small-business development.

In the end, programs run collaboratively with locals will achieve long-term, self-sustaining change. Wherever possible, reliance on projects run unilaterally by foreigners should be minimized.

The success of Turkey and other emerging market nations—as well as impressive gains in global health and microfinance—point to new models of assistance. The EU accession processes' impact on Turkey shows the value of creating economic incentives for local leaders to carry out reform. Congress could offer duty-free, quota-free access to U.S. markets to Middle Eastern countries transitioning to democracy. An expanded economic union involving the

United States, Europe, and certain countries in the region could be created, again using the model of the EU and Turkey. Or the United States could sign free-trade agreements with individual countries. Enterprise funds that encourage investment in the region by U.S. companies could be expanded as well.

Across the region, trade and investment should be wielded as tools of long-term American influence. Predominantly Muslim countries should no longer be viewed solely through the lens of counterterrorism. Instead, policy makers should adopt the Acumen Fund's concept of "patient capital" and a "third way." Poverty cannot be eliminated by the market alone. Nor can government solely eradicate it.

The only arena where the Unites States has demonstrated a willingness to meet international challenges with adequate resources has been the military. The Pentagon bureaucracy dwarfs the civilian bureaucracy. Worldwide, the State Department fields twelve thousand Foreign Service officers. Each day, twenty-three thousand people—nearly twice that number—go to work at the Pentagon. If we are serious about reimagining American influence and security, we must make equivalent investments in institutions that promote diplomacy, development, and trade. The American military—the largest government organization in the United States—invests massively in training its personnel. Civilian agencies should do the same.

In its second term, the Obama administration must reprioritize those agencies, adequately fund them, and support their efforts politically. In particular, USAID must be reconstituted. Top-level expertise, authority, and salaries should reside within the agency, not with private contractors. And instead of issuing massive contracts, the agency should create smaller, more nimble long-term initiatives that could be implemented by smaller organizations and adapted to changing circumstances. Reducing the size and cost of projects will make them easier to shield from demands for immediate results, and more sustainable over the long term.

Entrepreneurship programs that leverage the popularity of Facebook, Apple, and other American tech companies should be increased. Fulbright and other educational programs should be massively expanded. Interacting with the region strengthens American security; it does not threaten it.

The goal should not be to hurl tens of billions of American taxpayer dollars at Tunisia, Egypt, Libya, and other countries. It should be to facilitate investment, education, and exchange over the long term. Doing fewer things over a longer period of time will prove more effective. Public-private partnerships, innovation, and revitalized civilian institutions are America's way forward.

In the end, the gravest threat to America's security is Washington's partisanship, feeble civilian institutions, and failure to match its ambitions with its actual resources and capabilities. The world is changing, but Washington is not.

Perhaps the most difficult task for the Obama administration will be responding to the rise of Islamist political parties across the region. Once outlawed, Islamist parties now hold power in Turkey, Tunisia, and Egypt. More victories are likely to follow.

American politicians and policy makers should be careful before considering Islamists enemies or allies. Islamists are deeply conservative and not moderates. Some view the West as unrelenting imperialists and blame every major development in the region on a hidden American hand. Others see the West as corrupt, materialistic, and in moral decay. Nearly all view the United States as unfairly pro-Israel. But if Islamists practice democratic norms, uphold international human rights, and win fair elections, their right to hold power should be respected.

Cutting off all international assistance to Islamists in post–Arab Spring countries, as the United States did to Hamas after its 2006 election victory, would be a mistake. The American cutoff—and the Israeli blockade of Gaza—allows Hamas to blame the suffering of Palestinians on Israel and the United States.

In private, American officials told me they hoped to create economic and political incentives that will make being part of the international system appealing to Islamists. That is the right course. Holding office and being responsible for creating prosperous economies, better government services, and less corruption will moderate Islamists. If they govern and fail, their popularity will erode. United States–backed crackdowns will only increase their support. In the end, Islamists who embrace democracy are more preferable than hard-line Salafists who embrace violence.

If Islamists abide by democratic and international norms, their right to participate in electoral politics should be respected. Believing in God and democracy is possible. An extraordinary debate about the very nature of Islam is unfolding across the Middle East. It is vital that Washington allows it to play out.

ACKNOWLEDGMENTS

This book would not have been possible without the brave work of scores of other journalists. As I described in the author's note at the beginning of this book, for personal reasons I have not traveled to Afghanistan, Pakistan, Egypt, or Libya since 2009. I fully acknowledge the enormous limitations this approach placed on my reporting. The goal of this book is to spark debate, not to serve as an encyclopedic history. My apologies for any of the book's many shortcomings. I take full responsibility for all mistakes, errors, and omissions.

I first want to thank the many brave people I met in South Asia and the Middle East who convinced me of this book's core thesis. Their belief in democracy, tolerance, and human rights while faced by violent attacks from Salafists deeply inspired me. They will win the historic struggle between moderates and extremists now convulsing the Islamic world. This book is my effort to help them.

More than any other individual, Jonathan Moore brought this book to fruition. He listened to my explanations for why I wanted to write it, counseled me on how best to do so, and then spent countless hours reading dismal drafts. His incisive comments and edits vastly improved the book. His encouragement was priceless. He is an extraordinary public servant, scholar, and friend. I am lucky to have him in my life.

My extraordinary editors at Thomson Reuters gave me an opportunity to become a columnist, allowed me to write this book, and made possible the travel it involved. This book would not have been possible without them. I thank Steven Adler, Paul Ingrassia, Chrystia Freeland, Jim Ledbetter, Paul Smalera, Allison Silver, Chadwick Matlin, and Joe Mandel. Chrystia and Jim, in particular, believed in this book and me. I am enormously grateful for all the help, encouragement, and inspiration they have given me.

Many other editors and reporters at Thomson Reuters supported this project as well and patiently waited when this book took up time, particularly Mike Williams, Stuart Karle, Alix Freedman, Jim Impoco, Kristina Cooke, and Deb Nelson.

More than any other colleague at Reuters, though, Missy Ryan, a friend and extraordinary journalist, provided insight into every aspect of this book. Her experience covering the fall of the Qaddafi regime in Libya, twenty months covering the war in Iraq, and the last two years covering American policy in Afghanistan and Pakistan have given her a unique perspective on the issues I have tried to address here. She was a constant source of encouragement and insight. My Reuters colleagues and friends Felix Salmon, Ben Walsh, Peter Rudegeair, and Uzra Khan have also been wonderful.

Editors at the *Atlantic* have been incredibly supportive and encouraging as well. For featuring my work I thank particularly David Bradley, James Bennet, Bob Cohn, John Gould, Derek Thompson, Max Fisher. Stories I wrote for Reuters and *Foreign Policy* magazine's Jim Impoco about drone warfare make up a chapter of this book. I am enormously grateful to Jim Impoco, Susan Glasser, and Blake Hounshell for their guidance, editing, and help.

A chapter I wrote about Richard Holbrooke for a 2011 book on his life, *The Unquiet American: Richard Holbrooke in the World*, serves as a chapter as well. My thanks to PublicAffairs, the publisher, as well as to my editors, Samantha Power and Derek Chollet, for their help, insight, and support.

Administrators and colleagues at Brown University were supportive as well when I taught a journalism class there while working on this book. I thank Ruth Simmons, Kevin McLaughlin, Mark Schlissel, David Kertzer, Stephen Foley, Lawrence Stanley, Elizabeth Taylor, Tracy Breton, Jonathan Readey, Marilyn Netter, Marianne Costa, Lorraine Mazza, and Ellen Viola. I thank Norman Boucher, Peter Andreas, and Michael Kennedy, and my students as well.

Many people helped with the reporting of this book. In New York, Suchi Mathur and Ruth Fecych provided invaluable research and guidance. Fred Abrahams, a senior associate with Human Rights Watch, who has been visiting Libya since 2005, provided insights into a country I have never visited. So did Youssef Gaigi, a Tunisian journalist who covered the Libyan uprising for Al Jazeera and his own new company, Tunisia Live.

In Egypt, Lauren E. Bohn conducted reporting for me on the ground and offered her valuable insights and advice. A Fulbright fellow, Overseas Press Club fellow, Pulitzer Center grantee, and assistant editor of the *Cairo Review*, Lauren was extraordinarily helpful, resourceful, and patient. Along with original reporting she did for me, I have quoted extensively from pieces she wrote for the Daily Beast, CNN, and other media. Dalia Mogahed's insights on Egypt and the region as a whole in the post–Arab Spring were enormously helpful as well.

The reporting of Elmira Bayrasli, an old friend from Bosnia, exposed me to the challenges entrepreneurs face in developing countries. She generously agreed that I could quote extensively from an excellent piece she wrote in the summer 2012 issue of the *World Policy Journal* that described two of the people in this book. Her forthcoming book *Steve Jobs Lives in Pakistan: Extraordinary Entrepreneurs in the Developing World* will be an even greater contribution to the topic.

In Tunisia, Youssef Gaigi, Zied Mhirsi, Farah Samti, and many others from Tunisia Live were incredibly helpful before, during, and after my reporting trip there.

In Turkey, Nevra Yarac and Selcuk Tepeli were incredible reporters, guides, and friends. In a second trip to Turkey, Syrian refugee Mahmoud Mosa helped me report in refugee camps and understand the tragedy unfolding in his country. The work of Erika Solomon and other Reuters colleagues who bravely reported in Syrian was invaluable.

In Afghanistan and Pakistan, the friendships and reporting of Carlotta Gall, Tim Golden, and Declan Walsh helped me tremendously, as did the work of many Afghan and Pakistani journalists whose names I will not mention for safety reasons. The Iraq chapter of this book is based entirely on reporting I did with my friend and colleague Michael Moss at the *New York Times*. He is an extraordinary journalist, person, and friend.

Along with teaching me journalism, the *Times* saved the lives of two Afghan journalists, Tahir Luddin and Asad Mangal, and me when we were kidnapped by the Taliban in November 2008. I will always regret what Tahir, Asad, and their families went through. I apologize to them and their families, and thank all of them for their tremendous understanding and bravery.

The *Times*'s tireless efforts over seven months to win our release convinced our captors that we were worth keeping alive. That gave us the opportunity to wait for a chance to escape. I thank Pakistan Army Major Nadeem Khattack for allowing us onto his military base in the middle of the night after Tahir and I escaped as our guard slept. Thanks to the efforts of the *Times* and Asad's family, Tahir returned home safely six weeks later.

ACKNOWLEDGMENTS

I will always be enormously grateful to Arthur Sulzberger Jr., Bill Keller, Jill Abramson, Dean Baquet, Susan Chira, John Geddes, William Schmidt, David McCraw, Matt Purdy, Christine Kay, and so many other longtime friends at the *Times* for their help in New York. They saved our lives.

In Afghanistan, Carlotta Gall, Chris Chivers, Adam Ellick, Rich Oppel, and my amazing Afghan colleagues and friends worked tirelessly to help us. In Pakistan, Ismail Khan, Salman Masood, Beena Sarwar, Pir Zubair Shah, Jane Perlez, and many others did as well. Their work on our behalf endangered them, and I will always be grateful for what they did.

Many other friends, experts, and officials helped enormously and devoted tremendous amounts of time, energy, and resources to our case, particularly Michael Semple, Richard Holbrooke, Kati Marton, Samantha Power, Karl and Ching Eikenberry, Marin Strmecki, Kay McGowan, Tim Golden, Michael Moss, and Peter Bergen.

Mark Mazzetti, Eric Schmitt, Douglas Franz, Ahmed Rashid, and Barbara Quinn provided generous expertise as well. I admire, respect, and salute the courage, sacrifice, and bravery of Sultan Munadi, Daniel Pearl, Piotr Stanczak, Bowe Bergdahl, and all journalists who remain in captivity.

I will always be enormously grateful to my editors and friends at the *Christian Science Monitor* who helped me when the Bosnian Serbs detained me for ten days in 1995. David Cook, Clayton Jones, Faye Bowers, and many others have my eternal gratitude.

The reporting, help, and friendship of many colleagues at the *New York Times* made this book possible and inspired and encouraged me for years. They include Anthony Shadid, Joe Kahn, David D. Kirkpatrick, Neil MacFarquhar, Anne Barnard, Tim Arango, David E. Sanger, Tyler Hicks, Dexter Filkins, Marcus Mabry, Roger Cohen, Graham Bowley, Rob Mackey, Scott Shane, Thom Shanker, Alissa

Rubin, Graham Bowley, Rod Nordland, Robert Worth, and many others. Earlier in my career, Chris Isham, Richard Greenberg, and Aram Roston gave me a chance and inspired me at ABC News. Paul Jablow and Linda Linley did the same at the *Philadelphia Inquirer.*

This book is filled with work of other journalists from across the Middle East and South Asia, including Rajiv Chandrasekaran, Ahmed Rashid, Josh Paltrow, Ken Dilanian, Adam Entous, Siobhan Gorman, Julian Barnes, Peter Finn, Greg Miller, Karen DeYoung, David Finkel, Dana Priest, Bob Woodward, James Dobbins, Seth Jones, Louisa Loveluck, Laura Rozen, Thomas Mann, William Dobson, Tarek Osman, Pratap Chatterjee, Milan Vaishnav, and Daniel Cutherell. Many current and former government officials in Washington and across the region helped me but wish to remain anonymous. I thank them as well.

Many friends helped me over the years while working on this book. Eric and Sylvan Wold, Julian Borger, Paul Salopek, Greg Scholl, Chloe Breyer, Marcello Picone, Ivan Obregon, Salman Ahmed, Elliot Thomson, Julian Borger, Kathleen Reen, Ivan Obregon, Lisa Ferrari, Kannan Sundaram, Don Nay, the Bissell family, Paul Haven, Victoria Burnett, Barry Bearak, Gary Bass, and George Packer have my thanks.

Emma Daly, Santiago Lyon, Stacy Sullivan, Laura Pitter, Jonathan Landay, Katie Moore, Kit Roane, Katya Jestin, Joel Brand, Ben Ward, Leigh Cheng, John Bastian, Pete Brandt, Al Erickson, Matt Borger, Rod Peterson, Damon Struyk, Jim Williamson, Bob Perkins, Steve Cote, Jim Webb, Jay, Joe and Doris Brenchick, and Rocky and Martha Manoriti do as well. Vincent Manoriti, Denise Morgan, Mary Anne Schwalbe, Sultan Munadi, and Peter Boisvert will always inspire me.

Last and most important, I thank the people who created this book. Sarah Chalfant has been a tireless friend, editor, and agent for more than fifteen years. I thank her for all she has done to make this book a reality. Editors at Viking took a risk on a book at a time when Americans have grown enormously tired of the region. I thank Clare Ferraro, Linda Cowen, Barbara Campo, Margaret Riggs, Randee Marullo, Jane Cavolina, and Josh Karpf, who patiently put up with rapidly changing events in the region and missed deadlines. Carolyn Coleburn, Bennett Petrone, and Meredith Burks did extraordinary work promoting the book as well.

My editor at Viking, Wendy Wolf, is more responsible for this book's existence than anyone else. She took research I had conducted for an initial book on Afghanistan and had the vision to turn it into something much more forward-looking. Our kidnapping seemed to end my dream of writing a book about the post-9/11 decade. Wendy resurrected that dream. I will always be enormously grateful to her. I could not have had a more patient, supportive, and insightful editor. I thank her for believing in this book.

Finally, I thank my family. My parents, Carol and Harvey; siblings Lee, Laura, and Erik; stepparents Andrea and George; and stepbrothers, Daniel and Joel; and many aunts, uncles, nieces, nephews, and cousins. They have showered me with love and have endured years of worry, and they all dropped everything and performed heroically—particularly Lee—when I needed them most. My in-laws—Jim and Mary Jane, Christie, Chris, Karen, Jason, Howard, and Christina—have put up with the same stresses for fewer years and given enormous support, love, and encouragement for a new family member.

My wife, Kristen, has endured more in four years of marriage than many spouses experience in a lifetime. She recognized the importance of this book and supported me throughout the reporting and writing of it. I thank her for her encouragement, patience, and love. Today I am living the life of my dreams. It is all because of her.

NOTES

INTRODUCTION

Page

xiii **and the spending of $1.2 trillion:** For a detailed accounting of spending since the 9/11 attacks, see Amy Belasco, *The Cost of Iraq, Afghanistan, and Other Global War on Terror Operations Since 9/11*, Congressional Research Service, March 29, 2011, http://www.fas.org/sgp/crs/natsec/RL33110.pdf.

xiv **in political life:** See Pew Research Center, *Most Muslims Want Democracy, Personal Freedoms, and Islam in Public Life*, July 10, 2012, http://www.pewglobal.org/2012/07/10/most-muslims-want-democracy-personal-freedoms-and-islam-in-political-life/.

xiv **ways of doing business:** See Pew Research Center, *Global Opinion of Obama Slips, International Policies Faulted*, June 13, 2012, http://www.pewglobal.org/2012/06/13/chapter-2-attitudes-toward-american-culture-and-ideas/.

xv **more than 100 million jobs will need to be created in the region by 2020:** See Sara Hamdan, "Jobs and Age Reign in Risk Factors for Mideast Uprisings," *New York Times*, February 2, 2011, http://www.nytimes.com/2011/02/03/world/middleeast/03iht-m03job.html?pagewanted=all.

xvi **95 percent:** See Belasco.

xvi **At the peak:** See Commission on Wartime Contracting, *Transforming Wartime Contracting: Controlling Costs, Reducing Risks: Final Report to Congress,* August 2011, 30–31, http://www.wartimecontracting.gov /docs/CWC_FinalReport-lowres.pdf.

xvi **was sometimes more costly:** Ibid., 39–40.

xvi **waste, fraud, and abuse:** Ibid., 2, 5.

CHAPTER 1: LITTLE AMERICA

3 **wean Afghans from Soviet influence:** See Cynthia Clapp-Wincek, *The Helmand Valley Project in Afghanistan,* USAID, December 1983, 1–3. The full report is a detailed history and assessment of the Helmand project.

3 **"Little America":** For elegant descriptions of cold war Lashkar Gah, see Arnold Toynbee, *Between Oxus and Jumna* (1961), and Nancy Hatch Dupree, *An Historical Guide to Afghanistan* (1977). For an exhaustive collection of the USAID-commissioned studies of the projects during the cold war, see Richard Scott, "Scott's Helmand Valley Archives," at www.scottshelmandvalleyarchives.org.

4 **loftier, long-term goals:** Louis Dupree is very critical of the project, particularly in its early phases; see Louis Dupree, *Afghanistan* (1970), 482–85, 497, 499–507, 634–35. Nick Cullather also criticizes the project; see Nick Cullather, "Damming Afghanistan: Modernization in a Buffer State," *Journal of American History* 89, no. 2 (September 2002): 512–37. For USAID descriptions of the project, see Lloyd Baron, *Sector Analysis: Helmand-Arghandab Valley Region,* USAID, February 1973, 2, 7–9; and Mildred Caudill, *Helmand-Arghandab Valley: Yesterday, Today, Tomorrow,* USAID, 1969, 31. Residents of Helmand and former USAID officials generally praised the project in interviews conducted in Afghanistan between 2004 and 2008 and in the United States between 2004 and 2012.

5 **Karakul fur:** See Cullather, 512–17.

8 **"We felt that we were free now":** See David Rohde, "An Afghan Symbol for Change, Then Failure," *New York Times,* September 5, 2006, http:// www.nytimes.com/2006/09/05/world/asia/05afghan.html.

10 **$130,000 a year:** Interviews with Grader and USAID officials in Afghanistan.

19 **Rory Donohoe:** See David Rohde, "Taliban Raise Poppy Production to

a Record Again," *New York Times,* August 26, 2007, http://www.nytimes .com/2007/08/26/world/asia/26heroin.html?pagewanted=all.

25 **In 2010, a series of studies:** See *Afghanistan Mortality Survey: 2010 Health Study Shows Significant Gains in Afghan Maternal and Child Health,* USAID, January 30, 2012, http://transition.usaid.gov/locations/ afghanistanpakistan/countries/afghanistan/ams2010.html.

26 **National Solidarity Program:** See *Afghanistan's National Solidarity Program Has Reached Thousands of Afghan Communities, but Faces Challenges That Could Limit Outcomes,* Office of the Special Inspector General for Afghanistan Reconstruction, March 22, 2011, www.sigar .mil/pdf/audits/2011-03-22audit-11-08.pdf.

26 **Ministry of Communications and Information Technology:** See Javid Hamdard, *The State of Telecommunications and Internet in Afghanistan: Six Years Later (2006–2012),* Internews, April 19, 2012, http://www.inter news.org/research-publications/state-telecommunications-and-internet-afghanistan-six-years-later-2006-2012.

27 **spent nearly $1.3 billion:** See Rajiv Chandrasekaran, "Cost of War in Afghanistan Will Be Major Factor in Troop-Reduction Talks," *Washington Post,* May 30, 2011, http://www.washingtonpost.com/world /national-security/cost-of-war-in-afghanistan-will-be-major-factor-in -troop-reduction-talks/2011/05/27/AGR8z2EH_print.html.

30 **shot dead an Afghan colleague:** See Abdul Malek, "South African Contractor Held for Killing Afghan Guard," Reuters, October 3, 2009, http:// www.reuters.com/article/2009/10/03/us-afghanistan-contractor-sb -idUSTRE5921HJ20091003.

30 **The *Washington Post* reported:** See Rajiv Chandrasekaran, "U.S. Pursues a New Way to Rebuild in Afghanistan," *Washington Post,* June 19, 2009, http://www.washingtonpost.com/wp-dyn/content/article/2009/ 06/18/AR2009061804135.html.

30 **systematic overbilling:** See Marisa Taylor and Warren P. Strobel, "U.S. Contractor Accused of Fraud Still Winning Big Afghan Projects," McClatchy, September 19, 2010, http://www.mcclatchydc.com/2010/09/19/ 100690/us-contractor-accused-of-fraud.html.

30 **pleaded guilty:** See "Husband and Wife Co-owners of Subcontracting Company Plead Guilty to Contract Fraud Related to Afghanistan Re-

building," Office of Public Affairs, Department of Justice, September 9, 2009, http://www.justice.gov/opa/pr/2009/September/09=crm=943 .html.

CHAPTER 2: LAW AND DISORDER IN IRAQ

32 **Jay Garner:** See Michael Moss and David Rohde, "Law and Disorder: Misjudgments Marred U.S. Plans for Iraqi Police," *New York Times,* May 21, 2006, http://www.nytimes.com/2006/05/21/world/middleeast/21 security.html?pagewanted=all; and Michael Moss, "Law and Disorder: How Iraq Police Reform Became a Casualty of War," *New York Times,* May 22, 2006, http://www.nytimes.com/2006/05/22/world/middleeast /22security.html?pagewanted=all.

35 **would be left to the Iraqi police:** Ibid.

35 **U.S. Army Lieutenant Colonel Robert Waltemeyer:** See David Rohde, "Deadly Unrest Leaves a Town Bitter at U.S.," *New York Times,* April 20, 2003, http://www.nytimes.com/2003/04/20/world/a-nation -at-war-mosul-deadly-unrest-leaves-a-town-bitter-at-us.html.

36 **Rumsfeld said:** See Moss and Rohde.

37 **he recalled:** Ibid.

43 **"The police are working":** Ibid.

43 **release in October 2013:** See Clem Richardson, "Bernie Kerik Copes with Prison Life," *New York Daily News,* June 13, 2012, http://articles .nydailynews.com/2012-06-13/news/32199756_1_bernie-kerik-hala -matli-bernard-kerik.

43 **in the next thirty days:** See Moss and Rohde (2006) and Moss (2006).

46 **"Some were just sitting":** Ibid.

46 **"qualified personnel":** Ibid.

48 **$1 billion:** See Business Wire, "DynCorp International Inc. to Be Ac-quired by Cerberus Capital Management, L.P.," April 12, 2010, http:// www.businesswire.com/news/home/20100412006033/en/DynCorp -International-Acquired-Cerberus-Capital-Management-L.P.

49 **sale of DynCorp:** Ibid.; and see Greg Roumeliotis, "McKeon, Founder of PE Firm Veritas, Committed Suicide," Reuters, September 14, 2012; http://www.reuters.com/article/2012/09/14/us-veritas-death-idUSBRE 88D1CS20120914.

CHAPTER 3: A CIVILIAN SURGE

50 **shuttering Guantánamo:** See Peter Finn, "Obama's Plan to Shutter Guantanamo Faces Hurdles," *Washington Post,* January 22, 2009, http://www.washingtonpost.com/wp-dyn/content/article/2009/01/21/AR 2009012101036.html.

50 **a robust civilian surge:** See David Rohde, "The Last Mission," in *The Unquiet American: Richard Holbrooke in the World,* ed. Derek Chollet and Samantha Power (2011), 282–83.

51 **and spanned five presidencies:** Ibid.; and see James Mann, *The Obamians* (2012), 229–40.

53 **he hired him as well:** See George Packer, "The Last Mission: Richard Holbrooke's Plan to Avoid the Mistakes of Vietnam in Afghanistan," *New Yorker,* September 28, 2009, http://m.newyorker.com/reporting /2009/09/28/090928fa_fact_packer?currentPage=all.

56 **AED, meanwhile, rode the:** See Dana Hedgpeth and Josh Boak, "USAID Suspends District-Based Nonprofit AED from Contracts amid Investigation," *Washington Post,* December 8, 2010, http://www.washingtonpost .com/wp-dyn/content/article/2010/12/08/AR2010120807665.html.

56 **pay back the government:** See "Washington, D.C.–Based Academy for Educational Development Pays More Than $5 Million to Settle False Claims Act Allegations," Office of Public Affairs, Department of Justice, June 30, 2011, http://www.justice.gov/usao/dc/news/2011/jun/11-278.pdf.

56 **was paid $879,530:** See Ken Dilanian, "Review: High Salaries for Aid Group CEOs," *USA Today,* September 1, 2009, http://www.usatoday .com/news/world/2009-08-31-us-aid-groups_N.htm#chart.

57 **"This dinner is over":** See Rajiv Chandrasekaran, *Little America* (2012), 89.

58 **could be cathartic:** Based on interviews with several former aides to Holbrooke and administration officials who agreed to speak with me only on condition that their names not be made public.

60 **would speak to Karzai:** Ibid.

60 **were plotting against him:** Ibid.

63 **"vital national security interests":** See Laurence Arnold, "Richard Holbrooke, U.S. Diplomat from Vietnam to Afghanistan, Dies Aged 69,"

Bloomberg, December 14, 2010, http://www.bloomberg.com/news/2010 -12-14/richard-holbrooke-u-s-diplomat-from-vietnam-to-afghanistan -dies-aged-69.html.

64 **"opposition from others"**: See Chollet and Power, 287.

66 **became a sign of progress**: See Chandrasekaran, 197–99.

66 **"If that money could have been spread out"**: Interviews and e-mail exchanges with Dempsey in 2011 and 2012.

67 **Holbrooke's insatiable ego**: Interviews with former administration officials and Holbrooke's aides.

67 **when Holbrooke was out of town**: See Chandrasekaran, 197–99.

67 **meeting between Karzai and Obama**: Ibid.

68 **that Holbrooke be included**: Ibid.

CHAPTER 4: THE RISE OF THE DRONE

69 **felt toward the United States**: See Chollet and Power, 291–93.

71 **calling the conditions "humiliating"**: See Omar Waraich, "How a U.S. Aid Package Could Threaten Zardari," *Time,* October 8, 2009, http:// www.time.com/time/world/article/0,8599,1929306,00.html.

72 **"reasonable period for the latter"**: See Laura Rozen, "Dissent Memo: USAID Official Charges Holbrooke Pakistan Aid Plan Flawed," *Politico,* October 12, 2009, http://www.politico.com/blogs/laurarozen/1009 /Dissent_Memo_USAID_official_charges_Holbrooke_Pakistan_aid _plan_flawed.html.

73 **respond to their requests quickly**: See Chollet and Power, 291–93.

75 **military ID cards, and a camera**: See Declan Walsh, "A CIA Spy, a Hail of Bullets, Three Killed and a US-Pakistan Diplomatic Row," *Guardian,* February 20, 2011, http://www.guardian.co.uk/world/2011/feb/20/cia-agent -lahore-civilian-deaths; and Asif Chaudhry, "US Official Guns Down Two Motorcyclists in Lahore," *Dawn,* January 28, 2011, http://dawn.com /2011/01/28/us-official-guns-down-two-motorcyclists-in-lahore/.

76 **Pakistani officials flatly disagreed**: See Greg Miller and Karen De-Young, "U.S., Pakistani Officials at Diplomatic Odds in Fatal Shooting," *Washington Post,* February 10, 2011, http://www.washingtonpost.com /wp-dyn/content/article/2011/02/09/AR2011020906436.html.

76 **working as a contractor for the CIA**: See Declan Walsh and Ewan Mac-

Askill, "American Who Sparked Diplomatic Crisis over Lahore Shooting Was CIA Spy," *Guardian,* February 20, 2011, http://www.guardian.co.uk/ world/2011/feb/20/us-raymond-davis-lahore-cia; and Mark Mazzetti, Ashley Parker, Jane Perlez, and Eric Schmitt, "American Held in Pakistan Worked with CIA," *New York Times,* February 21, 2011, http://www.ny times.com/2011/02/22/world/asia/22pakistan.html?pagewanted=all.

76 **American intelligence agencies were contractors:** See Dana Priest and William M. Arkin, "A Hidden World, Growing Beyond Control," *Washington Post,* July 19, 2010, http://projects.washingtonpost.com/top -secret-america/articles/a-hidden-world-growing-beyond-control/.

77 **scale up the size of the organization:** Ibid.

77 **rapidly increase its workforce:** Ibid.

77 **eight years in prison:** See Agence France-Presse, "Court Upholds CIA Contractor's Detainee Abuse Conviction," August 11, 2009, http://www .google.com/hostednews/afp/article/ALeqM5gSo6iRtgbNNlDhDyO _VcZEmT45MQ.

78 **"fuel our cars and run our factories":** See Macon Phillips, "President Barack Obama's Inaugural Address," The White House, January 21, 2009, http://www.whitehouse.gov/blog/inaugural-address.

78 **created instability, not stability:** See David Rohde, "The Obama Doctrine: How the President's Drone War Is Backfiring," *Foreign Policy,* March/April 2012, http://www.foreignpolicy.com/articles/2012/02/27 /the_obama_doctrine?page=full.

80 **thirty-three drone strikes in total:** Ibid.

80 **The CIA quickly killed the plan:** Ibid.; interviews with former administration officials; and see Dennis C. Blair, "Drones Alone Are Not the Answer," *New York Times,* August 14, 2012, http://www.nytimes.com /2011/08/15/opinion/drones-alone-are-not-the-answer.html.

80 **ignored Munter's protests:** See Adam Entous, Siobhan Gorman, and Julian E. Barnes, "U.S. Tightens Drone Rules," *Wall Street Journal,* November 4, 2011, http://online.wsj.com/article/SB10001424052970204621 904577013982672973836.html.

81 **Davis was released on March 16:** See *BBC,* "Pakistan Anger over Release of CIA Killer Raymond Davis," March 17, 2011, www.bbc.co.uk /news/world-south-asia-12769714.

81 **over a bagel shop parking spot:** See Lee Ferran, "Raymond Davis, CIA Contractor, Charged with Felony in Parking Lot Skirmish," ABC News, October 4, 2011, http://abcnews.go.com/Blotter/raymond-davis-cia -contractor-charged-parking-lot-fight/story?id=14663216.

81 **an unusual public statement:** See Sebastian Abbot, "Pakistan Army Chief Condemns US Drone Attack," Associated Press, March 17, 2011, http://o.seattletimes.nwsource.com/html/nationworld/2014522314 _apaspakistan.html.

81 **"not a charity car wash":** Ibid.

82 **more than twenty people:** Interviews with former administration officials; and see *Dawn*, "Rare Condemnation by PM, Army Chief: 40 Killed in Drone Attack," March 18, 2011, http://dawn.com/2011/03/18/rare -condemnation-by-pm-army-chief-40-killed-in-drone-attack/; and Entous, Gorman, and Barnes.

82 **over the signature strikes:** See Entous, Gorman, and Barnes.

83 **during the same period in 2010:** See Counterterrorism Strategy Initiative, *The Year of the Drone: An Analysis of U.S. Drone Strikes in Pakistan, 2004–2012*, New American Foundation, August 24, 2012, http://counter terrorism.newamerica.net/drones.

83 **to review the attacks:** See Dianne Feinstein, "Letters: Sen. Feinstein on Drone Attacks," *Los Angeles Times,* May 17, 2012, http://articles.latimes .com/2012/may/17/opinion/la-le-0517-thursday-feinstein-drones -20120517.

83 **a 14-percentage-point rise from 2008:** See Pew Global Attitudes Project, *Pakistani Public Opinion Ever More Critical of U.S.* (Overview), Pew Research Center, June 27, 2012, http://www.pewglobal.org/2012/06/27 /pakistani-public-opinion-ever-more-critical-of-u-s/; and Pew Global Attitudes Project, *Pakistani Public Opinion Ever More Critical of U.S.* (Chapter 1: Views of the U.S. And American Foreign Policy), Pew Research Center, June 27, 2012, http://www.pewglobal.org/2012/06/27 /chapter-1-views-of-the-u-s-and-american-foreign-policy-5/.

87 **the challenges entrepreneurs face:** See Elmira Bayrasli, "Entrepreneurs Save the World," *World Policy Journal,* Summer 2012, http://www .worldpolicy.org/journal/summer2012/entrepreneurs-save-the-world.

CHAPTER 5: WHERE ISLAM AND DEMOCRACY MEET, UNEASILY

93 **the country's disenfranchised Shiite majority:** "Arab Spring, Fall, and After," *New York Times,* February 21, 2012, http://www.nytimes.com/ interactive/2011/11/23/world/middleeast/Arab-Spring-and-Fall.html.

94 *Milliyet* **wrote:** See Tim Arango and Hwaida Saad, "Turkey's Parliament Backs Military Measures on Syria," *New York Times,* October 4, 2012, http://www.nytimes.com/2012/10/05/world/middleeast/syria.html ?pagewanted=all.

94 **40-million-strong middle class:** See World Factbook, *Country Comparison: GDP—Real Growth Rate 2012,* Central Intelligence Agency (accessedAugust 29, 2012), https://www.cia.gov/library/publications/the -world-factbook/rankorder/2003rank.html?countryName=Turkey &countryCode=tu&regionCode=mde&rank=15#tu.

94 **to silence dissent:** See Dexter Filkins, "The Deep State," *New Yorker,* March 12, 2012, http://www.newyorker.com/reporting/2012/03/12/1203 12fa_fact_filkins.

95 **political repression:** See David Rohde, "Where Islam and Democracy Meet, Uneasily," Reuters, October 21, 2011, http://www.reuters.com /article/2011/10/21/idUS209035153320111021.

95 **was frequent:** See David Rohde, "The Islamic World's Culture War, Played Out on TV Soap Operas," *Atlantic,* March 9, 2012, http://www .theatlantic.com/international/archive/2012/03/the-islamic-worlds -culture-war-played-out-on-tv-soap-operas/254247/.

96 **"a negative light":** See Ece Toksabay and Ibon Villelabeitia, "Sultan's TV Drama Opens Turkish Divide on Religion," Reuters, February 8, 2011, http://www.reuters.com/article/2011/02/08/us-turkey-ottoman -drama-idUSTRE7173GA20110208.

96 **toned down:** See Rohde, "The Islamic World's Culture War, Played Out on TV Soap Operas."

96 **a phenomenal hit:** See Robert F. Worth, "Arab TV Tests Societies' Limits with Depictions of Sex and Equality," *New York Times,* September 26, 2008, http://www.nytimes.com/2008/09/27/world/middleeast/27beirut .html.

97 **85 million viewers:** See AMEinfo.com, "Beirut Hosts the 2nd New Arab Woman Forum (NAWF)," September 11, 2008, http://www.ameinfo .com/168434.html.

97 **and groundbreaking:** See Worth.

97 **divorces occurred in several countries:** See Al Arabiya News, "Turkish Soap Star Sparks Divorces in Arab World," June 29, 2008, http://www .alarabiya.net/articles/2008/06/29/52291.html.

97 **Islamic clerics denounced *Noor*:** See Andy Sambidge, "MBC Expands Soap Opera Shows Despite Mufti Fury," *Arabian Business,* October 21, 2008, http://www.arabianbusiness.com/mbc-expands-soap-opera-shows -despite-mufti-fury-84564.html; and Worth.

98 **received glowing coverage:** See Nadia Bilbassy-Charters, "Leave It to Turkish Soap Operas to Conquer Hearts and Minds," *Foreign Policy,* April 15, 2010, http://mideast.foreignpolicy.com/posts/2010/04/15 /leave_it_to_turkish_soap_operas_to_conquer_hearts_and_minds; and Owen Matthews, "The Arab World's 'Dallas,'" *Newsweek,* September 5, 2011, http://www.thedailybeast.com/newsweek/2011/09/04/turkish -soap-operas-are-sweeping-the-middle-east.html.

98 **the Coen brothers of Turkey:** See Rohde, "The Islamic World's Culture War, Played Out on TV Soap Operas."

98 **victory tour of the region:** See Rohde, "Where Islam and Democracy Meet, Uneasily."

99 **"can run a state very successfully":** See Cecile Feuillatre, "Buoyant Erdogan Sells Turkish Model to Arab Spring," Agence France-Presse, September 14, 2012, http://www.google.com/hostednews/afp/article/ALeq M5iYbCJEmBCnS-3bEXWY9mkdKHxSwA.

100 **drafted after a 1980 military coup:** See Rohde, "Where Islam and Democracy Meet, Uneasily."

101 **in emerging market countries:** See Bayrasli.

101 **wireless routers designed for American drywall:** Ibid.

104 **a source of stability for Turkey:** See Rohde, "Where Islam and Democracy Meet, Uneasily."

104 **Syrian refugees accepted by Turkey:** See Stephanie Nebehay, "Syrian Refugees in Turkey Could Top 200,000: U.N.," Reuters, August 28, 2012, http://news.yahoo.com/syrians-fleeing-jordan-could-herald

-much-larger-influx-093714760.html; and Arango and Saad, October 4, 2012.

105 **Europe followed a clear set of policies:** See Bartlomiej Kaminski and Francis Ng, *Turkey's Evolving Trade Integration into Pan-European Markets: World Bank Policy Research Working Paper 3908*, World Bank, May 2006.

CHAPTER 6: THE SILICON VALLEY OF THE ARAB WORLD?

106 **"Muslim communities around the world":** See "Remarks by the President on a New Beginning," Office of the Press Secretary, The White House, June 4, 2009, http://www.whitehouse.gov/the-press-office /remarks-president-cairo-university-6-04-09.

107 **officials thought the uprisings:** See David E. Sanger, *Confront and Conceal: Obama's Secret Wars and Surprising Use of American Power* (2012), 283–88.

107 **for training and mentoring:** See David Rohde, "Can Tunisia Become the Silicon Valley of the Arab World?," *Atlantic*, March 30, 2012, http:// www.whitehouse.gov/the-press-office/remarks-president-cairo-university-6-04-09.

109 **A 2012 survey found that:** See Pew Global Attitudes Project, *Most Muslims Want Democracy, Personal Freedoms, and Islam in Political Life*.

109 **growth it enjoyed between 1997 and 2007:** See Daniel Loehr, "IMF Recommends a Control on Public Expenditures," *Tunisia Live*, August 6, 2012, http://www.tunisia-live.net/2012/08/06/imf-recommends-a -control-on-public-expenditures/.

111 **that unnerved Tunisian moderates:** See Ahmed Ellali, "Several Thousand Salafists Demonstrate for Islamic Law, Attack Dramatists in Tunis," *Tunisia Live*, March 25, 2012, http://www.tunisia-live.net /2012/03/25/several-thousand-salafists-demonstrate-for-islamic-law-attack-dramatists-in-tunis/; and Tarek Amara and Lin Noueihed, "Tunisian Salafi Islamists Riot over 'Insulting' Art," Reuters, June 12, 2012, http://www.reuters.com/article/2012/06/12/us-tunisia-salafis-clash -idUSBRE85B0XW20120612; and Pesha Magid, "Union of Journalists Condemns Proposed Limits on Freedom of Press," *Tunisia Live*, August 8, 2012, http://www.tunisia-live.net/2012/08/08/union-of-journalists

-condemns-proposed-limits-on-freedom-of-the-press/; and Paul Schemm, "Tunisian Democracy Threatened by Weak Opposition," Associated Press, July 4, 2012, http://bigstory.ap.org/article/tunisian-democracy-threatened-weak-opposition.

111 **in the style of Afghan Taliban:** See Bouazza Ben Bouazza and Paul Schemm, "Tunisian Radicals Travel to Syria," Associated Press, June 21, 2012, http://bigstory.ap.org/article/tunisian-radicals-travel-syria.

117 **the 2011 G8 summit in Deauville:** See Patrick Wintour, "G8 Summit to Pledge £12bn for Arab Spring States," *Guardian,* May 27, 2011, http://www.guardian.co.uk/world/2011/may/27/g8-summit-pledge-arab-spring.

CHAPTER 7: MURDER IN BENGHAZI

123 **wrote stories about him:** See David Corn and Siddhartha Mahanta, "From Libya with Love," *Mother Jones,* March 3, 2011, http://www.motherjones.com/politics/2011/03/libya-qaddafi-monitor-group; and Ed Pilkington, "The Monitor Group: Gaddafi's PR Firm Used Academics," *Guardian,* March 4, 2011, http://www.guardian.co.uk/world/2011/mar/04/the-monitor-group-gadaffi-pr.

123 **Qaddafi's son's, Saif:** See Chris Cook, "Davis Blamed over Gaddafi's Gift to LSE," *Financial Times,* December 1, 2011, http://www.ft.com/intl/cms/s/0/4971e882-1b63-11e1-85f8-00144feabdc0.html#axzz250YSEoCM.

123 **Obama can stay forever:** See Mark Sappenfield and Tracey Samuelson, "Qaddafi UN Speech: Six Highlights—or Lowlights?" *Christian Science Monitor,* September 23, 2009, http://www.csmonitor.com/USA/Politics/The-Vote/2009/0923/qaddafi-un-speech-six-highlights-or-lowlights.

125 **information provided by the Libyan government:** See Rod Nordland and Scott Shane, "Libyan, Once a Detainee, Is Now a U.S. Ally of Sorts," *New York Times,* April 24, 2011, http://www.nytimes.com/2011/04/25/world/guantanamo-files-libyan-detainee-now-us-ally-of-sorts.html.

125 **blocked detainees from seeing judges:** See Fred Abrahams, "Libya Slogs Toward Democracy," *Daily Beast,* July 24, 2012, http://www.the

dailybeast.com/articles/2012/07/24/with-gaddafi-gone-libya-slogs
-toward-democracy.html.

126 **independent candidates:** Ibid.

127 **told the *New York Times*:** See Eric Schmitt, David D. Kirkpatrick, and Suliman Ali Zway, "U.S. May Have Put Mistaken Faith in Libya Site's Security," *New York Times,* October 1, 2012, http://www.nytimes.com/2012/10/01/world/africa/mistaken-sense-of-security-cited-before-envoy-to-libya-died.html?pagewanted=all.

127 **Islamic militants:** Ibid.

128 **armed Libyan fighters:** Ibid.

129 **American-made anti-Muslim video:** David Rohde, "Honoring a Slain Ambassador," Reuters, September 13, 2012, http://blogs.reuters.com/david-rohde/2012/09/13/honoring-a-slain-ambassador/.

129 **"would have wanted that":** Ibid.

130 **"there's the door!":** See Embassy of the United States, Tripoli, Libya, "Remarks by Ambassador Chris Stevens at the Reopening of the Consular Section," August 26, 2012, http://libya.usembassy.gov/en_082612.html.

CHAPTER 8: POST-MUBARAK

131 **Gallup poll:** Dalia Mogahed, "Opinion Briefing: Egyptians Skeptical of U.S. Intentions," Gallup World, September 21, 2012, http://www.gallup.com/poll/157592/opinion-briefing-egyptians-skeptical-intentions.aspx.

132 **61 percent of Egyptians:** See Pew Global Attitudes Project, *Egyptians Remain Optimistic, Embrace Democracy and Religion in Political Life,* Pew Research Center, May 8, 2012, http://www.pewglobal.org/2012/05/08/chapter-5-views-of-the-united-states-and-israel/.

133 **a healthy 5.1 percent before the uprising:** See Michael Schuman, "Why the New Egyptian President's Biggest Worry Could Be the Economy," *Time,* June 27, 2012, http://business.time.com/2012/06/27/why-the-new-egyptian-presidents-biggest-worry-could-be-the-economy/.

133 **Egypt's foreign currency reserves:** See David D. Kirkpatrick, "Struggling, Egypt Seeks Loan from IMF," *New York Times,* January 16, 2012, http://www.nytimes.com/2012/01/17/world/middleeast/egypt-seeks-3-2-billion-loan-from-imf.html.

133 **tourism revenue:** See Ahmed Namatalla and Alaa Shahine, "Egypt Current Account Deficit Widens as Tourism, FDI Fall," Bloomberg, June 10, 2012, www.bloomberg.com/news/2012-06-10/egypt-current -account-deficit-widens-as-tourism-fdi-fall-1-.html.

134 **youth unemployment:** Reporting by Lauren E. Bohn; and see Lauren E. Bohn and Tim Lister, "The Key to Liberating Egyptians? The Economy," CNN, June 29, 2012, http://articles.cnn.com/2012-06-29/middleeast /world_meast_egypt-economy_1_muslim-brotherhood-egyptians -khairat. And for a detailed description of Egypt's revolution and the political dynamics at work in the country, see William J. Dobson, *The Dictator's Learning Curve* (2012), 187–23.

134 **in August 2012:** See *BBC*, "Egypt Leader Mursi Orders Army Chief Tantawi to Resign," August 12, 2012, http://www.bbc.co.uk/news /world-africa-19234763.

134 **El Erian:** See Ahmed Eleiba, "Brotherhood's El-Erian Believes Rapprochement with Iran, Hamas in Egypt's Interest," Ahram Online, September 20, 2012, http://english.ahram.org.eg/NewsContentPrint/1/0/53411/Egypt /0/QA-Brotherhoods-ElErian-believes-rapprochement-wit.aspx.

138 **cooperation between Egyptian and American scientists:** The narrative on U.S. assistance to Egypt since Camp David comes from Jeremy M. Sharp, *Egypt: Transition Under Military Rule,* Congressional Research Service, June 21, 2012, 14–24, http://fpc.state.gov/documents/ organization/194799.pdf.

138 **secretly fomented the antigovernment protests:** See Robert Mackey, "Behind Jeers for Clinton in Egypt, a Conspiracy Theory with U.S. Roots, *New York Times,* July 16, 2012, http://thelede.blogs.nytimes.com /2012/07/16/egyptians-who-jeered-clinton-cite-american -conservatives-to-argue-u-s-secretly-supports-islamists/.

139 **nonpartisan workshops on political organizing:** See David D. Kirkpatrick and Steven Lee Meyers, "Scramble Is On to Find Deal for 16 Americans in Egypt," *New York Times,* February 25, 2012, http://www .nytimes.com/2012/02/26/world/middleeast/us-seeks-deal-for -americans-facing-charges-in-egypt.html.

140 **"The revolution gave people":** See Bohn and Lister, "The Key to Liberating Egyptians? The Economy."

143 "'I want to be an entrepreneur'": Lisa Katayama, "How Anna Elliot's Bamyan Media Used Reality TV to Help Entrepreneurs in Afghanistan," *Fast Company,* October 13, 2010, http://www.fastcompany.com/1694476/how-anna-elliots-bamyan-media-used-reality-tv-help-entrepreneurs-afghanistan.

144 **a source of instability:** Louisa Loveluck, *Education in Egypt: Key Challenges,* Chatham House, March 2012, http://www.chathamhouse.org/sites/default/files/public/Research/Middle%20East/0312egyptedu_background.pdf; and reporting by Lauren Bohn; and see Lauren Bohn, "Egypt, as Protests Rage, School Begins," *Daily Beast,* September 15, 2012; http://www.thedailybeast.com/articles/2012/09/15/egypt-as-protests-rage-school-begins.html.

144 **Sweeping economic inequality:** Ibid.

144 **challenge colonial rule:** Ibid.

145 **quality of higher education plummeted:** Ibid.

145 **widespread gender inequality:** Ibid.

145 **80 percent are literate:** Ibid.; and World Factbook, Egypt, https://www.cia.gov/library/publications/the-world-factbook/geos/eg.html.

145 **standardized tests, not critical thinking:** Bohn and Loveluck.

146 **in exchange for cash:** Ibid.

146 **said Osman:** Osman was interviewed in Egypt by Lauren E. Bohn; see also Tarek Osman, *Egypt on the Brink: From Nasser to Mubarak* (2011).

147 **to be an engineer:** See Lauren E. Bohn, "For Egypt's Trapped and Teeming, Revolution Has Barely Begun," CNN, June 7, 2012, http://www.cnn.com/2012/06/07/world/africa/egypt-next-revolution/index.html.

147 **and a potential bride:** Ibid.

147 **passage into adulthood:** Ibid.

CHAPTER 9: LITTLE WASHINGTON

150 **surprised, thrilled, and inspired:** Interviews with Koltai, July and August 2012.

156 **investor in the sector:** Retrieved from Carlyle Group Web site, August 2012, http://carlyle.com/.

157 **after the 9/11 attacks:** Ibid.

157 **as much as $2 billion each:** Ibid.

159 **$554 million in government contracts:** See *Washington Technology,* "2012 Top 100 Rankings," June 11, 2012, http://washingtontechnology .com/toplists/top-100-lists/2012.aspx.

159 **chief innovation officer:** Interview with O'Neill, August 2012.

161 **long-term policies:** Interview with Chaudhary, August 2012.

162 **Micah Zenko:** See Paul B. Stares, John Vessey, and Micah Zenko, *Enhancing U.S. Preventive Action,* Council on Foreign Relations, New York, October 2009, http://www.cfr.org/conflict-prevention/enhancing -us-preventive-action/p20378; and Paul B. Stares and Micah Zenko, *Partners in Preventive Action,* Council on Foreign Relations, New York, September 2011, http://www.cfr.org/international-organizations/partners -preventive-action/p25938?co=C009603.

162 **the problem was leadership:** See David E. Sanger, *Confront and Conceal* (2012), 417–27.

CONCLUSION

164 **executing members:** See *BBC,* "Syria Conflict: Aleppo Shooting by Rebels Condemned," August 1, 2012, http://www.bbc.co.uk/news/world -middle-east-19084287.

165 **he told Reuters:** See Erika Solomon, "Insight: Syria Rebels See Future Fight with Foreign Radicals," Reuters, August 8, 2012, http://www .msnbc.msn.com/id/48564227/ns/world_news-mideastn_africa/.

170 **short-term energy needs:** See Nancy Birdsall, Milan Vaishnav, and Daniel Cutherell, *More Money, More Problems: A 2012 Assessment of the US Approach to Development in Pakistan,* Center for Global Development, July 30, 2012, http://www.cgdev.org/content/publications/detail /1426361/; and Milan Vaishnav, *Washington's Civilian Shortcomings in Pakistan,* Carnegie Endowment, July 31, 2012, http://carnegieendowment.org/2012/07/30/washington-s-civilian-shortcomings-in-pakistan/d34p; and Shuja Nawaz, "Stilling a Stormy Relationship," *Foreign Policy,* July 12, 2012, http://afpak.foreignpolicy.com/posts /2012/07/12/stilling_a_stormy_relationship.

BIBLIOGRAPHY

The list below includes articles, books, documents, and reports that I read fully, read partially, or consulted. I am deeply indebted to the courageous work of journalists in the countries I have not visited since 2009: Afghanistan, Pakistan, Libya, and Egypt.

ARTICLES

Abbot, Sebastian. "Pakistan Army Chief Condemns US Drone Attack." Associated Press, March 17, 2011. http://o.seattletimes.nwsource.com/html/nationworld/2014522314_apaspakistan.html.

Abrahams, Fred. "Libya Slogs Toward Democracy." *Daily Beast,* July 24, 2012. http://www.thedailybeast.com/articles/2012/07/24/with-gaddafi-gone-libya-slogs-toward-democracy.html.

Agence France-Presse. "Court Upholds CIA Contractor's Detainee Abuse Conviction." August 11, 2009. http://www.google.com/hostednews/afp/article/ALeqM5gSo6iRtgbNNlDhDyO_VcZEmT45MQ.

Al Arabiya News. "Turkish Soap Star Sparks Divorces in Arab World." June 29, 2008. http://www.alarabiya.net/articles/2008/06/29/52291.html.

Amara, Tarek, and Lin Noueihed. "Tunisian Salafi Islamists Riot over 'Insulting' Art." Reuters, June 12, 2012. http://www.reuters.com/article/2012/06/12/us-tunisia-salafis-clash-idUSBRE85B0XW20120612.

AMEinfo.com. "Beirut Hosts the 2nd New Arab Woman Forum (NAWF)." September 11, 2008. http://www.ameinfo.com/168434.html.

Arango, Tim, and Hwaida Saad. "Turkey's Parliament Backs Military Measures on Syria," New York Times, October 4, 2012. http://www.nytimes.com/2012/10/05/world/middleeast/syria.html?pagewanted=1&hp&pagewanted=all.

Arnold, Laurence. "Richard Holbrooke, U.S. Diplomat from Vietnam to Afghanistan, Dies Aged 69." Bloomberg, December 14, 2010. http://www.bloomberg.com/news/2010-12-14/richard-holbrooke-u-s-diplomat-from-vietnam-to-afghanistan-dies-aged-69.html.

Bayrasli, Elmira. "Entrepreneurs Save the World." World Policy Journal, Summer 2012. http://www.worldpolicy.org/journal/summer2012/entrepreneurs-save-the-world.

BBC. "Pakistan Anger over Release of CIA Killer Raymond Davis." March 17, 2011. www.bbc.co.uk/news/world-south-asia-12769714.

———. "Syria Conflict: Aleppo Shooting by Rebels Condemned." August 1, 2012. http://www.bbc.co.uk/news/world-middle-east-19084287.

———. "Egypt Leader Mursi Orders Army Chief Tantawi to Resign." August 12, 2012. http://www.bbc.co.uk/news/world-africa-19234763.

Ben Bouazza, Bouazza, and Paul Schemm. "Tunisian Radicals Travel to Syria." Associated Press, June 21, 2012. http://bigstory.ap.org/article/tunisian-radicals-travel-syria.

Bilbassy-Charters, Nadia. "Leave It to Turkish Soap Operas to Conquer Hearts and Minds." Foreign Policy, April 15, 2010. http://mideast.foreignpolicy.com/posts/2010/04/15/leave_it_to_turkish_soap_operas_to_conquer_hearts_and_minds.

Blair, Dennis C. "Drones Alone Are Not the Answer." New York Times, August 14, 2012. http://www.nytimes.com/2011/08/15/opinion/drones-alone-are-not-the-answer.html.

Bohn, Lauren E. "Egypt, as Protests Rage, School Begins." Daily Beast, September 15, 2012. http://www.thedailybeast.com/articles/2012/09/15/egypt-as-protests-rage-school-begins.html.

———. "For Egypt's Trapped and Teeming, Revolution Has Barely Begun." CNN, June 7, 2012. http://www.cnn.com/2012/06/07/world/africa/egypt-next-revolution/index.html.

———, and Tim Lister. "The Key to Liberating Egyptians? The Economy." CNN, June 29, 2012. http://articles.cnn.com/2012-06-29/middleeast /world_meast_egypt-economy_1_muslim-brotherhood-egyptians -khairat.

Buccianti, Alexandra. "Dubbed Turkish Soap Operas Conquering the Arab World: Social Liberation or Cultural Alienation?" *Arab Media & Society,* Spring 2010. http://www.arabmediasociety.com/?article=735.

Business Wire. "DynCorp International Inc. to Be Acquired by Cerberus Capital Management, L.P." April 12, 2010. http://www.businesswire .com/news/home/20100412006033/en/DynCorp-International -Acquired-Cerberus-Capital-Management-L.P.

Chandrasekaran, Rajiv. "Cost of War in Afghanistan Will Be Major Factor in Troop-Reduction Talks." *Washington Post,* May 30, 2011. http://www .washingtonpost.com/world/national-security/cost-of-war-in -afghanistan-will-be-major-factor-in-troop-reduction-talks/2011/05/27 /AGR8z2EH_print.html.

———. "U.S. Pursues a New Way to Rebuild in Afghanistan." *Washington Post,* June 19, 2009. http://www.washingtonpost.com/wp-dyn/content /article/2009/06/18/AR2009061804135.html.

Chaudhry, Asif. "U.S. Official Guns Down Two Motorcyclists in Lahore." *Dawn,* January 28, 2011. http://dawn.com/2011/01/28/us-official-guns -down-two-motorcyclists-in-lahore/.

Cook, Chris. "Davis Blamed over Gaddafi's Gift to LSE." *Financial Times,* December 1, 2011. http://www.ft.com/intl/cms/s/0/4971e882-1b63-11e1 -85f8-00144feabdc0.html#axzz250YSEoCM.

Corn, David, and Siddhartha Mahanta. "From Libya with Love." *Mother Jones,* March 3, 2011. http://www.motherjones.com/politics/2011/03 /libya-qaddafi-monitor-group.

Cullather, Nick. "Damming Afghanistan: Modernization in a Buffer State." *Journal of American History* 89, no. 2 (September 2002): 512–37. http:// www.nyu.edu/gsas/dept/icas/Cullather.pdf.

Dawn. "Rare Condemnation by PM, Army Chief: 40 Killed in Drone At- tack." March 18, 2011. http://dawn.com/2011/03/18/rare-condemnation -by-pm-army-chief-40-killed-in-drone-attack/.

Dilanian, Ken. "Review: High Salaries for Aid Group CEOs." *USA Today,*

September 1, 2009. http://www.usatoday.com/news/world/2009-08-31 -us-aid-groups_N.htm#chart.

Eleiba, Ahmed. "Brotherhood's El-Erian Believes Rapprochement with Iran, Hamas in Egypt's Interest." Ahram Online, September 20, 2012. http:// english.ahram.org.eg/NewsContentPrint/1/0/53411/Egypt/0/QA -Brotherhoods-ElErian-believes-rapprochement-wit.aspx.

Ellali, Ahmed. "Several Thousand Salafists Demonstrate for Islamic Law, Attack Dramatists in Tunis." Tunisia Live, March 25, 2012. http://www .tunisia-live.net/2012/03/25/several-thousand-salafists-demonstrate-for -islamic-law-attack-dramatists-in-tunis/.

Entous, Adam, Siobhan Gorman, and Julian E. Barnes. "U.S. Tightens Drone Rules." Wall Street Journal, November 4, 2011. http://online .wsj.com/article/SB10001424052970204621904577013982672973836 .html.

Feinstein, Dianne. "Letters: Sen. Feinstein on Drone Attacks." Los Angeles Times, May 17, 2012. http://articles.latimes.com/2012/may/17/opinion /la-le-0517-thursday-feinstein-drones-20120517.

Ferran, Lee. "Raymond Davis, CIA Contractor, Charged with Felony in Parking Lot Skirmish." ABC News, October 4, 2011. http://abcnews.go .com/Blotter/raymond-davis-cia-contractor-charged-parking-lot-fight /story?id=14663216.

Feuillatre, Cecile. "Buoyant Erdogan Sells Turkish Model to Arab Spring." Agence France-Presse, September 14, 2012. http://www.google.com /hostednews/afp/article/ALeqM5iYbCJEmBCnS-3bEXWY9mkd KHxSwA.

Filkins, Dexter. "The Deep State." New Yorker, March 12, 2012. http://www .newyorker.com/reporting/2012/03/12/120312fa_fact_filkins.

Finn, Peter. "Obama's Plan to Shutter Guantanamo Faces Hurdles." Washington Post, January 22, 2009. http://www.washingtonpost.com/wp-dyn /content/article/2009/01/21/AR2009012101036.html.

Gall, Carlotta, and David Rohde. "Militants Escape Control of Pakistan, Officials Say." New York Times, January 15, 2008. www.nytimes.com/2008 /01/15/world/asia/15isi.html.

Hedgpeth, Dana, and Josh Boak. "USAID Suspends District-Based Nonprofit AED from Contracts amid Investigation." Washington Post, December 8,

2010. http://www.washingtonpost.com/wp-dyn/content/article/2010/12/08/AR2010120807665.html.

Katayama, Lisa. "How Anna Elliot's Bamyan Media Used Reality TV to Help Entrepreneurs in Afghanistan." *Fast Company*, October 13, 2010. http://www.fastcompany.com/1694476/how-anna-elliots-bamyan-media-used-reality-tv-help-entrepreneurs-afghanistan.

Kirkpatrick, David D. "Struggling, Egypt Seeks Loan from IMF." *New York Times*, January 16, 2012. http://www.nytimes.com/2012/01/17/world/middleeast/egypt-seeks-3-2-billion-loan-from-imf.html.

———, and Steven Lee Meyers. "Scramble Is On to Find Deal for 16 Americans in Egypt." *New York Times*, February 25, 2012. http://www.nytimes.com/2012/02/26/world/middleeast/us-seeks-deal-for-americans-facing-charges-in-egypt.html.

Lohr, Daniel. "IMF Recommends a Control on Public Expenditures." *Tunisia Live*, August 6, 2012. http://www.tunisia-live.net/2012/08/06/imf-recommends-a-control-on-public-expenditures/.

Mackey, Robert. "Behind Jeers for Clinton in Egypt, a Conspiracy Theory with U.S. Roots." *New York Times*, July 16, 2012. http://thelede.blogs.nytimes.com/2012/07/16/egyptians-who-jeered-clinton-cite-american-conservatives-to-argue-u-s-secretly-supports-islamists/.

Magid, Pesha. "Union of Journalists Condemns Proposed Limits on Freedom of Press." *Tunisia Live*, August 8, 2012. http://www.tunisia-live.net/2012/08/08/union-of-journalists-condemns-proposed-limits-on-freedom-of-the-press/.

Malek, Abdul. "South African Contractor Held for Killing Afghan Guard." Reuters, October 3, 2009. http://www.reuters.com/article/2009/10/03/us-afghanistan-contractor-sb-idUSTRE5921HJ20091003.

Matthews, Owen. "The Arab World's 'Dallas.'" *Newsweek*, September 5, 2011. http://www.thedailybeast.com/newsweek/2011/09/04/turkish-soap-operas-are-sweeping-the-middle-east.html.

Mazzetti, Mark, Ashley Parker, Jane Perlez, and Eric Schmitt. "American Held in Pakistan Worked with CIA." *New York Times*, February 21, 2011. http://www.nytimes.com/2011/02/22/world/asia/22pakistan.html?pagewanted=all.

———, and David Rohde. "Amid U.S. Policy Disputes, Qaeda Grows in Pakistan." *New York Times,* June 30, 2008. http://www.nytimes.com/2008 /06/30/washington/30tribal.html.

Miller, Greg, and Karen DeYoung. "U.S., Pakistani Officials at Diplomatic Odds in Fatal Shooting." *Washington Post,* February 10, 2011. http:// www.washingtonpost.com/wp-dyn/content/article/2011/02/09 /AR2011020906436.html.

Moss, Michael. "Law and Disorder: How Iraq Police Reform Became a Casualty of War." *New York Times,* May 22, 2006. http://www.nytimes.com /2006/05/22/world/middleeast/22security.html?pagewanted=all.

Moss, Michael, and David Rohde. "Misjudgments Marred U.S. Plans for Iraqi Police." *New York Times,* May 21, 2006. http://www.nytimes .com/2006/05/21/world/middleeast/21security.html?pagewanted=all.

Namatalla, Ahmed, and Alaa Shahine. "Egypt Current Account Deficit Widens as Tourism, FDI Fall." Bloomberg, June 10, 2012. http://www .bloomberg.com/news/2012-06-10/egypt-current-account-deficit-widens -as-tourism-fdi-fall-1-.html.

Nawaz, Shuja. "Stilling a Stormy Relationship." *Foreign Policy,* July 12, 2012. http://afpak.foreignpolicy.com/posts/2012/07/12/stilling_a_stormy _relationship.

Nebehay, Stephanie. "Syrian Refugees in Turkey Could Top 200,000: U.N." Reuters, August 28, 2012. http://news.yahoo.com/syrians-fleeing-jordan -could-herald-much-larger-influx-093714760.html.

New York Times. "Arab Spring, Fall, and After." February 21, 2012. http:// www.nytimes.com/interactive/2011/11/23/world/middleeast/Arab -Spring-and-Fall.html.

Nordland, Rod, and Scott Shane. "Libyan, Once a Detainee, Is Now a U.S. Ally of Sorts." *New York Times,* April 24, 2011. http://www.nytimes .com/2011/04/25/world/guantanamo-files-libyan-detainee-now-us-ally -of-sorts.html.

Packer, George. "The Last Mission: Richard Holbrooke's Plan to Avoid the Mistakes of Vietnam in Afghanistan." *New Yorker,* September 28, 2009. http://m.newyorker.com/reporting/2009/09/28/090928fa_fact_ packer?currentPage=all.

Pilkington, Ed. "The Monitor Group: Gaddafi's PR Firm Used Academics."

Guardian, March 4, 2011. http://www.guardian.co.uk/world/2011/mar
/04/the-monitor-group-gadaffi-pr.

Priest, Dana, and William M. Arkin. "A Hidden World, Growing Beyond
Control." *Washington Post,* July 19, 2010. http://projects.washingtonpost
.com/top-secret-america/articles/a-hidden-world-growing-beyond
-control/.

Richardson, Clem. "Bernie Kerik Copes with Prison Life." *New York Daily
News,* June 13, 2012. http://articles.nydailynews.com/2012-06-13
/news/32199756_1_bernie-kerik-hala-matli-bernard-kerik.

Rohde, David. "An Afghan Symbol for Change, Then Failure." *New York
Times,* September 5, 2006. www.nytimes.com/2006/09/05/world/asia
/05afghan.html.

———. "Can Tunisia Become the Silicon Valley of the Arab World?" *Atlantic,*
March 30, 2012. http://www.whitehouse.gov/the-press-office/remarks-
president-cairo-university-6-04-09.

———. "Deadly Unrest Leaves a Town Bitter at U.S." *New York Times,* April
20, 2003. http://www.nytimes.com/2003/04/20/world/a-nation-at-war
-mosul-deadly-unrest-leaves-a-town-bitter-at-us.html.

———. "Held by the Taliban." *New York Times,* October 17–21, 2009. http://
www.nytimes.com/2009/10/18/world/asia/18hostage.html.

———. "Honoring a Slain Ambassador." Reuters, September 13, 2012. http://
blogs.reuters.com/david-rohde/2012/09/13/honoring-a-slain
-ambassador/.

———. "The Islamic World's Culture War, Played Out on TV Soap Operas."
Atlantic, March 9, 2012. http://www.theatlantic.com/international
/archive/2012/03/the-islamic-worlds-culture-war-played-out-on-tv
-soap-operas/254247/.

———. "The Obama Doctrine: How the President's Drone War Is Backfiring." *Foreign Policy,* March/April 2012. http://www.foreignpolicy.com
/articles/2012/02/27/the_obama_doctrine?page=full.

———. "Taliban Raise Poppy Production to a Record Again." *New York
Times,* August 26, 2007. http://www.nytimes.com/2007/08/26/world
/asia/26heroin.html?pagewanted=all.

———. "Where Islam and Democracy Meet, Uneasily." Reuters, October 21,

2011. http://www.reuters.com/article/2011/10/21/idUS2090351533201110 21.

——, and David E. Sanger, "How a Good War Went Bad in Afghanistan." *New York Times,* August 12, 2007. www.nytimes.com/2007/08/12/world /asia/12afghan.html?pagewanted=all.

——, Carlotta Gall, Eric Schmitt, and David E. Sanger. "U.S. Officials See Waste in Billions Sent to Pakistan." *New York Times,* December 24, 2007. http://www.nytimes.com/2007/12/24/world/asia/24military .html?pagewanted=all.

Rozen, Laura. "Dissent Memo: USAID Official Charges Holbrooke Pakistan AID Plan Flawed." *Politico,* October 12, 2009. http://www.politico.com /blogs/laurarozen/1009/Dissent_Memo_USAID_official_charges_Hol brooke_Pakistan_aid_plan_flawed.html.

Sambidge, Andy. "MBC Expands Soap Opera Shows Despite Mufti Fury." *Arabian Business,* October 21, 2008. http://www.arabianbusiness.com /mbc-expands-soap-opera-shows-despite-mufti-fury-84564.html.

Sappenfield, Mark, and Tracey Samuelson. "Qaddafi UN Speech: Six High- lights—or Lowlights?" *Christian Science Monitor,* September 23, 2009. http://www.csmonitor.com/USA/Politics/The-Vote/2009/0923/qaddafi -un-speech-six-highlights-or-lowlights.

Schemm, Paul. "Tunisian Democracy Threatened by Weak Opposition." As- sociated Press, July 4, 2012. http://bigstory.ap.org/article/tunisian -democracy-threatened-weak-opposition.

Schmitt, Eric, David Kirkpatrick, and Suliman Ali Zway. "U.S. May Have Put Mistaken Faith in Libya Site's Security." *New York Times,* October 1, 2012. http://www.nytimes.com/2012/10/01/world/africa/mistaken-sense- of-security-cited-before-envoy-to-libya-died.html?pagewanted=all.

Schuman, Michael. "Why the New Egyptian President's Biggest Worry Could Be the Economy." *Time,* June 27, 2012. http://business.time. com/2012/06/27/why-the-new-egyptian-presidents-biggest-worry -could-be-the-economy/.

Shelton, Tracey. "Libya's Media Has Its Own Revolution." *GlobalPost,* March 18, 2012. http://www.globalpost.com/dispatch/news/regions /africa/120301/libya-media-revolution-newspapers-television-radio -journalism-free-speech.

Solomon, Erika. "Insight: Syria Rebels See Future Fight with Foreign Radicals." Reuters, August 8, 2012. http://www.msnbc.msn.com/id/48564227/ns/world_news-mideastn_africa/.

Taylor, Marisa, and Warren P. Strobel. "U.S. Contractor Accused of Fraud Still Winning Big Afghan Projects." McClatchy, September 19, 2010. http://www.mcclatchydc.com/2010/09/19/100690/us-contractor-accused-of-fraud.html.

Toksabay, Ece, and Ibon Villelabeitia. "Sultan's TV Drama Opens Turkish Divide on Religion." Reuters, February 8, 2011. http://www.reuters.com/article/2011/02/08/us-turkey-ottoman-drama-idUSTRE7173GA20110208.

Vardi, Nathan. "Wall Street Goes to War." Forbes, August 3, 2009. http://www.forbes.com/forbes/2009/0803/iraq-afghanistan-obama-wall-street-goes-to-war.html.

Walsh, Declan, and Ewan MacAskill. "A CIA Spy, a Hail of Bullets, Three Killed and a US-Pakistan Diplomatic Row." Guardian, February 20, 2011. http://www.guardian.co.uk/world/2011/feb/20/cia-agent-lahore-civilian-deaths.

———, and Ewan MacAskill. "American Who Sparked Diplomatic Crisis over Lahore Shooting Was CIA Spy." Guardian, February 20, 2011. http://www.guardian.co.uk/world/2011/feb/20/us-raymond-davis-lahore-cia.

Waraich, Omar. "How a U.S. Aid Package Could Threaten Zardari." Time, October 8, 2009. http://www.time.com/time/world/article/0,8599,1929306,00.html.

Washington Technology. "2012 Top 100 Rankings." June 11, 2012. http://washingtontechnology.com/toplists/top-100-lists/2012.aspx.

Wintour, Patrick. "G8 Summit to Pledge £12bn for Arab Spring States." Guardian, May 27, 2011. http://www.guardian.co.uk/world/2011/may/27/g8-summit-pledge-arab-spring.

Worth, Robert F. "Arab TV Tests Societies' Limits with Depictions of Sex and Equality." New York Times, September 26, 2008. http://www.nytimes.com/2008/09/27/world/middleeast/27beirut.html.

Zaalouk, Malak. "Now, the Education Revolution." Cairo Review of Global Affairs, August 29, 2012. http://www.aucegypt.edu/GAPP/CairoReview/Pages/articleDetails.aspx?aid=214.

BOOKS

Chandrasekaran, Rajiv. *Little America: The War Within the War for Afghanistan*. New York: Knopf, 2012.

Chatterjee, Pratap. *Iraq, Inc.: A Profitable Occupation*. New York: Seven Stories Press, 2004.

Chollet, Derek, and Samantha Power. *The Unquiet American: Richard Holbrooke in the World*. New York: PublicAffairs, 2011.

Dobson, William J. *The Dictator's Learning Curve: Inside the Global Battle for Democracy*. New York: Doubleday, 2012.

Dupree, Louis. *Afghanistan*. Oxford: Oxford University Press, 1973.

Dupree, Nancy Hatch. *An Historical Guide to Afghanistan*. Kabul: Afghan Tourist Organization, 1977.

Mann, James. *The Obamians: The Struggle Inside the White House to Redefine American Power*. New York: Viking, 2012.

Osman, Tarek. *Egypt on the Brink: From Nasser to Mubarak*. New Haven: Yale University Press, 2011.

Poullada, Leon B., and D. J. Leila. *The Kingdom of Afghanistan and the United States: 1828–1973*. Omaha and Lincoln, NE: The Center for Afghanistan Studies at the University of Nebraska at Omaha and Dageforde Publishing, 1995.

Rashid, Ahmed. *Descent into Chaos: The United States and the Failure of Nation Building in Pakistan, Afghanistan and Central Asia*. New York: Viking, 2008.

———. *Pakistan on the Brink: The Future of America, Pakistan and Afghanistan*. New York: Viking, 2012.

———. *Taliban: Militant Islam, Oil and Fundamentalism in Central Asia*. New Haven: Yale University Press, 2000.

Sanger, David E. *Confront and Conceal: Obama's Secret Wars and Surprising Use of American Power*. New York: Crown, 2012.

———. *The Inheritance: The World Obama Confronts and the Challenges to American Power*. New York: Crown, 2009.

Shook, Lucy. *Letters from Afghanistan*. Liz Adair, Ruth Lavine, and Terry Gifford, eds. Ferndale, WA: GAL Editing & Publishing, 2002.

Singer, P. W. *Corporate Warriors: The Rise of the Privatized Military Industry.* Ithaca, NY: Cornell University Press, 2003.

Toynbee, Arnold. *Between Oxus and Jumna.* Oxford: Oxford University Press, 1961.

Woodward, Bob. *Bush at War.* New York: Simon & Schuster, 2002.

———. *Obama's Wars.* New York: Simon & Schuster, 2010.

———. *Plan of Attack.* New York: Simon & Schuster, 2004.

———. *State of Denial.* New York: Simon & Schuster, 2006.

———. *The War Within.* New York: Simon & Schuster, 2008.

DOCUMENTS AND REPORTS

Baron, Lloyd. *Sector Analysis: Helmand-Arghandab Valley Region.* Kabul: United States Agency for International Development, 1973.

Belasco, Amy. *The Cost of Iraq, Afghanistan, and Other Global War on Terror Operations Since 9/11.* Washington, DC: Congressional Research Service, 2011. http://www.fas.org/sgp/crs/natsec/RL33110.pdf.

Birdsall, Nancy, Milan Vaishnav, and Daniel Cutherell. *More Money, More Problems: A 2012 Assessment of the US Approach to Development in Pakistan.* Washington, DC: Center for Global Development, 2012. http://www.cgdev.org/content/publications/detail/1426361/.

Caudill, Mildred. *Helmand-Arghandab Valley: Yesterday, Today, Tomorrow.* Lashkar Gah: United States Agency for International Development, 1969.

Clapp-Wincek, Cynthia. *The Helmand Valley Project in Afghanistan.* Washington, DC: United States Agency for International Development, 1983.

Commission on Wartime Contracting. *Transforming Wartime Contracting: Controlling Costs, Reducing Risks: Final Report to Congress.* Washington, DC: Government Printing Office, 2011. http://www.wartimecontracting.gov/docs/CWC_FinalReport-lowres.pdf.

Counterterrorism Strategy Initiative. *The Year of the Drone: An Analysis of U.S. Drone Strikes in Pakistan, 2004–2012.* Washington, DC: New American Foundation, 2012.

Dobbins, James, et al. *America's Role in Nation-Building: From Germany to Iraq.* Santa Monica, CA: RAND, 2003.

Embassy of the United States, Tripoli, Libya. "Remarks by Ambassador

Chris Stevens at the Reopening of the Consular Section," 2012. http://libya.usembassy.gov/en_082612.html.

Hamdard, Javid. *The State of Telecommunications and Internet in Afghanistan: Six Years Later (2006–2012)*. Washington, DC: Internews, 2012. http://www.internews.org/research-publications/state-telecommunications-and-internet-afghanistan-six-years-later-20062012.

Kaminski, Bartlomiej, and Francis Ng. *Turkey's Evolving Trade Integration into Pan-European Markets: World Bank Policy Research Working Paper 3908*. Washington, DC: World Bank, 2006.

Loveluck, Louisa. *Education in Egypt: Key Challenges*. London: Chatham House, 2012. http://www.chathamhouse.org/sites/default/files/public/Research/Middle%20East/0312egyptedu_background.pdf.

Moore, Jonathan. *Morality and Foreign Policy*. Hanover, NH: The Dickey Center, 2007. http://counterterrorism.newamerica.net/drones.

Office of the Press Secretary. "Remarks by the President on a New Beginning." Washington, DC: The White House, 2009. http://www.whitehouse.gov/the-press-office/remarks-president-cairo-university-6-04-09.

Office of Public Affairs. "Husband and Wife Co-owners of Subcontracting Company Plead Guilty to Contract Fraud Related to Afghanistan Rebuilding." Washington, DC: Department of Justice, 2009. http://www.justice.gov/opa/pr/2009/September/09-crm-943.html.

———. "Washington, D.C.–Based Academy for Educational Development Pays More Than $5 Million to Settle False Claims Act Allegations." Washington, DC: Department of Justice, 2011. http://www.justice.gov/usao/dc/news/2011/jun/11-278.pdf.

Office of the Special Inspector General for Afghanistan Reconstruction. *Afghanistan's National Solidarity Program Has Reached Thousands of Afghan Communities, but Faces Challenges That Could Limit Outcomes*. Washington, DC: Government Printing Office. 2011. http://www.sigar.mil/pdf/audits/2011-03-22audit-11-08.pdf.

Pew Global Attitudes Project. *Egyptians Remain Optimistic, Embrace Democracy and Religion in Political Life*. Washington, DC: Pew Research Center, 2012. http://www.pewglobal.org/2012/05/08/chapter-5-views-of-the-united-states-and-israel/.

———. *Most Muslims Want Democracy, Personal Freedoms, and Islam in Po-*

litical Life. Washington, DC: Pew Research Center, 2012. http://www
.pewglobal.org/2012/07/10/chapter-8-tunisias-relationship-with-the-u-s/.

———. *Pakistani Public Opinion Ever More Critical of U.S.* Washington, DC:
Pew Research Center, 2012. http://www.pewglobal.org/2012/06/27
/pakistani-public-opinion-ever-more-critical-of-u-s/.

Phillips, Macon. "President Barack Obama's Inaugural Address." Washington, DC: The White House Blog, 2009. http://www.whitehouse.gov/blog
/inaugural-address.

Sharp, Jeremy M. *Egypt: Transition Under Military Rule*. Washington, DC:
Congressional Research Service, 2012. http://fpc.state.gov/documents/
organization/194799.pdf.

Stares, Paul B., John Vessey, and Micah Zenko. *Enhancing U.S. Preventive
Action*. New York: Council on Foreign Relations, October 2009.

———, and Micah Zenko. *Partners in Preventive Action*. New York: Council
on Foreign Relations, September 2011.

United States Agency for International Development. *Afghanistan Mortality
Survey: 2010 Health Study Shows Significant Gains in Afghan Maternal
and Child Health*. Washington, DC: Government Printing Office, 2012.
http://transition.usaid.gov/locations/afghanistanpakistan/countries
/afghanistan/ams2010.html.

Vaishnav, Milan. *Washington's Civilian Shortcomings in Pakistan*. Washington, DC: Carnegie Endowment, 2012. http://carnegieendowment
.org/2012/07/30/washington-s-civilian-shortcomings-in-pakistan/d34p.

World Factbook. *Country Comparison: GDP—Real Growth Rate 2012*. Langley,
VA: Central Intelligence Agency, 2012. https://www.cia.gov/library/publica
tions/the-world-factbook/rankorder/2003rank.html?countryName=Turkey
&countryCode=tu&regionCode=mde&rank=15#tu.

INDEX

CREDITS

Portions of this book first appeared as "The Last Mission" in *The Unquiet American: Richard Holbrooke in the World*, Derek Chollet and Samantha Power, editors (Public Affairs, 2011), and "The Obama Doctrine: How the President's Drone War Is Backfiring," *Foreign Policy*, issue of February 27, 2012.

Grateful acknowledgment is made for permission to reprint the following works by David Rohde (or excerpts therefrom):

The New York Times: "In Newly Occupied Mosul, U.S. Colonel Faces 1.7 Million Added Responsibilities," issue of April 13, 2003; "Misjudgments Marred U.S. Plans for Iraqi Police" (by Michael Moss and David Rohde), May 21, 2006; "An Afghan Symbol for Change, Then Failure," September 5, 2006; "Taliban Raise Poppy Production to a Record Again," August 26, 2007; and "Personal Diplomacy," December 26, 2010. © 2003, 2006, 2007, 2010 The New York Times. All rights reserved. Used by permission and protected by the copyright laws of the United States. The printing, copying, redistribution, or retransmission of this content without express written permission is prohibited.

Reuters: "Where Islam and Democracy Meet, Uneasily," issue of October 21, 2011; "Talk for Now in Syria but Prepare to Arm," February 24, 2012; "Inside Islam's Culture War," March 8, 2012; "The Arab World's Silicon Valley?" March 30, 2012; "The Islamist Spring," April 5, 2012; "Little America: An Afghan town, an American Dream and the Folly of For-Profit War," June 1, 2012; "Honoring a Slain Ambassador," September 13, 2012; "Republicans Betray their Foreign Policy Tradition," September 19, 2012; "A Hidden Cause of Benghazi Tragedy," November 16, 2012; and "Morsi's Folly," November 23, 2012. Reprinted by arrangement with Reuters.